"You take the blue pill...
believe whatever you w[ant]...
in Wonderland; and [...]
— MORPHEUS T[...]

the
Debt
Millionaire

Most people will never build real wealth.
Now you can be one of the few who do.

GEORGE ANTONE

THE DEBT MILLIONAIRE
By George Antone
www.TheDebtMillionaireBook.com

FIRST EDITION

© 2016 by George Antone. All rights reserved.

No part of this book may be reproduced or transmitted in any form or by any electronic or mechanical means, including information storage and retrieval systems, without permission in writing from the publisher, except by a reviewer who may quote brief passages in a review.

Printed in the United States of America

Book design by The 750 Shop
Cover by Alejandro Espinosa

Events in the book have been fictionalized for educational content and impact.

ISBN-10:0982704534
ISBN-13:978-0-9827045-3-0

This publication is designed to provide information with regard to the subject matter covered. It is sold with the understanding that the publisher and author are not engaged in rendering investment, real estate, legal, accounting, tax, or other professional services and that the publisher and author are not offering such advice in this publication. If real estate, legal, or other expert assistance is required, the services of a competent, professional person should be sought. The publisher and author specifically disclaim any liability that is incurred from the use or application of the contents of this book.

This book is dedicated
to my children
Emile, Amanda and Christine
"I Vol U"

:-)

Table of Contents

Acknowledgments vii

Tools and Resources ix

The Inspiration of This Book xi

CHAPTER ONE: Introduction 3

CHAPTER TWO: The Wealth Equation 7

CHAPTER THREE:
The Traditional Method of Investing Doesn't Work! 15

CHAPTER FOUR: Hacking the System 31

CHAPTER FIVE: Moving to the Receiving Side of Interest 41

CHAPTER SIX:
Moving to the Receiving Side of Opportunity Cost! 53

CHAPTER SEVEN: Moving to the Receiving Side of Inflation 75

CHAPTER EIGHT: Lowering Your Taxes 99

CHAPTER NINE: Debt Revisited 111

CHAPTER TEN: The Third Secret Side—The Key to Wealth 117

CHAPTER ELEVEN: The Last & Most Important Leverage 133

CHAPTER TWELVE: The Family Bank 141

CHAPTER THIRTEEN: Putting it All Together 157

Epilogue 165

Appendix: A Few Debt Metrics 167

Resources 173

Acknowledgments

Years ago, when I first decided to write books I had no idea that my writing could or would change lives. I have seen people change their financial lives and futures because of the information I shared with them. For me there is truly no greater joy than knowing that I have changed the trajectory of people's lives, their family's lives, and then the lives of the people they in turn helped. What a blessing.

It is for you, the people that will use this information and change your lives that I continue to write these books and share my knowledge. Thank you for allowing me to share this information with you.

This book would not have been possible without the help of Swanee Heidberg, Bob Leeper, Clark Cordner, Alejandro Espinosa, and everyone at FYNANC LLC. Thank you so much.

Tools and Resources

We created a web site loaded with various free resources designed to help illustrate many of the concepts you will find in this book.

The resources on this web site were designed to enhance your learning experience.

Please visit the website for more information.

www.TheDebtMillionaireBook.com

The Inspiration of This Book

A special person passed away many years ago.

He had worked very hard to teach me about
wealth and success.

He always said (and showed me) that money was
meant to help others in need.

One of the many lessons he taught
me went something like this…

*"Make gravity work for you, not against you.
Make the system work for you, not against you."*

These insightful words would eventually change
everything I knew about "wealth."

This book is the result of that one lesson… as you will discover.

This book is for you from him.

His name was Emile.

He was my dad.

Section One

Introduction

Chapter One

Introduction

What if everything you know about investing is wrong?

What if the way you think and approach investing is wrong?

Why is it that as of 2010, the top 1% of households in the United States owned 35.4% of all privately held wealth?

Is there something you are missing?

Indeed there is!

"They" (the top 1%) own a "weapon" that they use to transfer all the wealth from most people (probably you too) onto their balance sheets, automatically, while you have NO IDEA it's being done!

It is not done illegally or with bad intention. It is simply the result of most people being ignorant or unaware of this "weapon".

Read this entire book.

Read it twice.

Welcome to "The Debt Millionaire."

It is time you opened your eyes!

It is time for you to learn about, and start using the same exact "weapon."

* * *

"George, what are you doing?" asked my mentor on the other end of the phone. "Want to drag along on a quick trip with me downtown?" He interjected before he allowed me to reply; "I'm coming over to pick you up" he chuckled, "be ready in 5. I'm on my way." "Um, okay. Where are we going?" I asked.

My mentor, a man ten years older than me, had built his fortune in real estate and real estate-related investments. For someone who was constantly mentioned in the news for his philanthropic work, he was very approachable and down to earth. He had his own financial challenges along the way with two bankruptcies and a hard upbringing. However, because of his tenacity, he went on to become one of the wealthiest people in San Jose, California.

"George, we are going to meet a friend of mine and I believe you will like this guy. I have learned a lot from him. Just listen carefully to him and think about everything he says. As you know, I'm not easily impressed with people, but you will like him" said my mentor again, as we sped down Almaden Expressway towards the freeway. I wasn't hearing much of what he was saying—I was worried for my life—he was driving fast!

I fastened my seat belt tightly and held on for dear life.

* * *

Imagine a "secret" investing method that changes your perspective on building wealth forever. Imagine this new method is an "automated" way to build wealth without trying hard. This method would not only shed light on why and how the very wealthy build wealth, but it would also explain how they "see" things very differently.

Would you want to know this "secret" investing method?

This book, in your hands right now, contains the information I learned about what is called "The WealthQ Method", a financial methodology based on something called "The Wealth Equation."

INTRODUCTION

Affluent families have used this method for centuries. They figured out a way to position themselves to build wealth automatically by simply flipping everything you know and believe about investing completely on its head. Historically, the results they obtained support using this system. In fact, by the end of this book, you should not just know of "The WealthQ Method" and "The Wealth Equation," but should also understand how the method works, and be convinced you cannot and should not build wealth any other way.

You will find yourself saying "wow—this is so true" and "this is so powerful" and then sit back in your seat and smile. I know this because I have shared this with people and that is exactly their reaction, time and time again.

Now, I want to share this story and this "secret" with you.

However, before I do, I want to explain to you my target audience for this book. This book is meant to be read by people who understand that wealth building includes the use of the right type of debt. If you are the type of person who listens to, agrees with, and believes the "gurus" on TV that talk about paying off your mortgages and being mortgage-free as being "the way", then perhaps this is not your "cup of tea." If you recognize that the use of debt CAN HELP you achieve your financial goals faster, but CAN ALSO DESTROY you if not used properly, then this book is a MUST read for you.

This book is not meant to be a "how to" book but rather a book that will help you think like the ultra-wealthy. Too many people are so indoctrinated they only want to read and follow "how to" books. I believe learning how to think (using your thinking capability) is much more important first than just learning the "how to".

Here is what I want you to be aware of and what I ask of you before you dive into the next section.

Promise yourself you will read this book all the way through.

Read it multiple times, if need be, to become comfortable with the Debt Millionaire concept.

I use numbers and math in a few places not to confuse you, but rather to share with you what I discovered along the way, and feel the excitement I experienced.

Hold on to your hat. This is going to be an exciting journey.

Everything you think you know about building wealth is about to be challenged.

* * *

"Look, the sign says 40 miles per hour" I uttered as I pointed out the window to the speed limit sign, while making sure he didn't see me sweat.

"George, I'm only going 50 miles per hour, so don't worry" he laughed.

"It feels like 100 miles per hour" I thought as I leaned over to look at the speedometer. He was right he was only going 50 but I was still scared nonetheless.

Chapter Summary

- The ultra-wealthy see wealth building in a very different way than everyone else.
- This book will introduce you to what the ultra-wealthy know and use a method called "The WealthQ Method" and it is based on "The Wealth Equation."
- You have to have an open mind when reading this book because it will challenge many things you believe to be true, no matter how many years of experience you have in investing.
- Read this book more than once.

Chapter Two

The Wealth Equation

We walked into the Il Fornaio restaurant in the Sainte Claire Hotel in downtown San Jose. The historic hotel gave a very classic feel to the restaurant.

As we approached a table, two men stood up to welcome my mentor and me. It was clear they were not expecting me, but we still exchanged pleasantries when my mentor introduced me. The older gentleman had snow white hair and looked like he was in his late 70s. Through his glasses, his brown eyes showed him to be a friendly and caring man. He wore a very expensive navy colored suit. Emile was his name. He commanded respect. Everyone in the restaurant was aware of him. The younger man, whom I found out later was his grandson, was in his early twenties, and wearing a light blue shirt with blue jeans. Emile was his name also, just like his grandfather.

After twenty minutes of "small talk" including ordering our drinks and food, my mentor brought up the topic that would change my life forever. This conversation would take several hours of this day, but the impact of that conversation would last me a lifetime.

"Emile, I would like to continue our conversation about the structured products you were talking to me about last week. But *before we begin could you please explain what you shared with me about 'The Wealth Equation' and 'The WealthQ Method' of investing to George first? You and he think alike. George will love the concept, and I'm sure he will put it to good use as well. He is a man that makes things happen" said my mentor.*

Emile looked at my mentor and then back at me and asked with a straight face "Are you married George?"

"Yes sir" I replied.

"Then let me share with you the secret formula for married couples." he said. Eager to learn, I grabbed a pen and opened my pad. "Okay, go for it" I smiled as I took a sip of my Arnold Palmer.

"Love One Another. And if that doesn't work, then bring the last word to the middle!"

I paused. I thought about what he had just said. I looked over to my mentor for a reaction. All four of us burst out laughing.

"Okay, I see you have a sense of humor George, so now I guess I can share with you the Wealth Equation." He smiled as he took a sip of his Cabernet Sauvignon.

"We call it the WealthQ" he said, "and the method of investing tied to this is called The WealthQ Method."

* * *

"The Wealth Equation" is the foundation of this book. In this chapter, I will share with you a high level overview and give you a basic explanation of the concept. For the rest of the book I will focus on and you will learn the details of the concept.

The Wealth Equation is also referred to as "WealthQ" and I will use these terms interchangeably throughout the book.

In the simplest terms "WealthQ" really boils down to one thing: <u>To build wealth, move to the right side of the equation.</u>

The Right Side of the Equation

Increasing your net-worth starts with you positioning yourself on the right side of the equation. A typical mathematical equation might look like this:

$$X + Y = Z$$

Assume these variables represent dollar amounts—money. That would mean the sum amount of X + Y dollars is the same as Z dollars. Or another way of looking at it—the money on the left side of the equation would be equal to the money on the right.

So if X is $6 and Y is $5, Z would be $11. Our equation would be:

$$X + Y = Z$$
$$\$6 + \$5 = \$11$$

In the real world, most people are on the left side of the equation—which is considered to be the "Paying" side. The right side of the equation is considered the "Receiving" side, and therefore must be equal to the left side. In other words, the left side is "paying" the right side.

The table below shows that James and Jill are on the "Paying" side of the equation, paying $2,000 and $3,000 respectively. Julia is on the "Receiving" side of the equation so she is receiving the $5,000.

PAYING SIDE	RECEIVING SIDE
$2,000 + $3,000	$5,000
James & Jill	**Julia**

TABLE 1: Paying Side versus Receiving Side

The equation looks like this:

$$\$2,000 + \$3,000 = \$5,000$$

(James & Jill pay Julia)

Obviously, we all want to be Julia in the example, but very few of us are.

In the real world, there are certain major "forces," and most people are (live) on the "Paying" side of these forces, as shown in the table below.

FORCE	PAYING SIDE	RECEIVING SIDE
Inflation	X	
Interest	X	
Taxes	X	
Opportunity Cost	X	

TABLE 2: Most People "Live" on the Paying Side of the "Forces"

The above table shows that most people are on the "Paying" side of inflation, interest, taxes and opportunity cost. As inflation rises, it affects them negatively. This table also shows that most people are on the paying side of interest, taxes and the biggest force, opportunity cost which will be explained in more detail later in the book.

If most people are on the "Paying" side of the major forces above, then who is on the "Receiving" side? The financial institutions and the ultra-wealthy are, as shown in the next table.

FORCE	PAYING SIDE	RECEIVING SIDE
Inflation	Most people	Federal Reserve System, ultra-wealthy
Interest	Most people	Federal Reserve System, Financial Institutions, ultra-wealthy
Taxes	Most people	Federal Government
Opportunity Cost	Most people	Federal Reserve System, Financial Institutions, ultra-wealthy

TABLE 3: Who "Lives" on the Right Side of Wealth Equation?

Yes, this is correct. As inflation goes up it affects the people on the right side positively. They increase their wealth automatically.

They are also on the receiving side of interest, and opportunity cost. The people on the right side cannot be on the receiving side of taxes, but they can and do focus on reducing taxes quite a bit.

So what does one have to do to become rich?

Simple!

Switch which side of the equation you're on. You want to position yourself to be on the right side of the equation (the WealthQ). Position yourself on the receiving end of those powerful forces. The following table illustrates your ideal goal.

FORCE	PAYING SIDE	RECEIVING SIDE
Inflation		You
Interest		You
Taxes	You Minimize	
Opportunity Cost		You

TABLE 4: YOUR GOAL IS TO MOVE TO THE RIGHT SIDE OF WEALTH EQUATION

Obviously, you can't be on the receiving end of taxes, but you can and should minimize how much you pay.

By simply moving yourself to the right side of the equation, you will start increasing your net-worth <u>automatically</u> while being on the same side as the financial institutions and the ultra-affluent.

This method of investing, focusing on moving to the "Receiving" side, is what's called "The WealthQ Method." Most people and investors are focusing on higher returns and "making more money". The WealthQ Method is a completely different, and I believe better, approach as you will soon find out. It is based on, and intended to move you to the right side of the WealthQ equation and make the system work for you instead of against you. Using the WealthQ Method you will end up investing in relatively safer assets than the people on the left side. You will have more liquidity (more capital in the bank), and build your net-worth faster than the people on the left side! On the right side the system works in your favor!

Throughout this book I intend to help you learn the WealthQ Method and how to move to the right side.

I like the following analogy.

Let's say you are flying an airplane (going through life) trying to get to your destination (your financial goals). Your airspeed is 200 miles per hour (you are investing as best you were taught) but there is a headwind (a force working against you) of 175 miles per hour. Your situation is such you will make only slow headway toward your destination (25 miles per hour in our example). Depending on the distance you need to travel and the time you have to travel, you may never reach you goal. This is a perfect example of being on the left side of the WealthQ with the headwinds (forces) working against you.

Now let's say you are flying an airplane (going through life) trying to get to your destination (your financial goals). Your airspeed is 200 miles per hour but you intelligently planned your flight path (learned all you could about moving to the right side of the WealthQ) and now as you fly along you have a tailwind (a force working for you) of 175 miles per hour. Your situation is such that you will make steady headway toward your destination. Because you understand how the plane and the tailwind (the force) work together you are in control. You can fly at 375 miles per hour or you can control and monitor your flight speed and time to reach your destination at a reasonable, safe (low risk and volatility), and controlled speed. This is why you want a tailwind, and exactly why you want the system working FOR you and not against you.

Headwinds and tailwinds (forces) are always there. They are a fact of nature. In the WealthQ the forces are always there. They are a result of how the system was built. Your ability to achieve your life's financial goals will be greatly enhanced by your learning, understanding and then applying the investment techniques necessary to have the forces in the WealthQ working to your advantage. Learn how to find that tailwind.

People and investors on the left side are trying really hard just to increase their returns, but they are still flying against the headwinds (the forces in the system). Their financial advisors give them advice attempting to make slightly better returns, but again, it doesn't change the fact they are still flying against those headwinds. Continuing to fly against those winds is not the answer. To succeed financially requires a complete change of perspective. Moving to the right side of the WealthQ equation and positioning yourself to allow the forces to work for you is key to your success.

Once you shift to the "Receiving" side of the WealthQ you have the tailwind on your side. The forces on the right side help you build wealth automatically. You are not working as hard, and wealth is building much easier.

The first step to recognize is this: To build wealth automatically, you have to learn how to switch to the right or "Receiving" side. It is just too difficult to build wealth from the left or "Paying" side!

The WealthQ Method is not about increasing returns or buying bigger assets, it is a complete change in perspective!

The WealthQ Method is not about increasing returns or buying bigger assets, it is a complete change in perspective! It's about making the system work for you.

In fact, most investors and advisors are so focused on returns they are completely missing the big picture. They are stuck on the "Paying" side and believe it's all about returns. They completely miss how people on the right side might have capital sitting in their checking account and be increasing their wealth more than their counterparts invested in various instruments on the "Paying" side.

This book will remove for you a lot of the "noise" out there about investing. It will help you understand what you need to do, and more importantly, how you need to THINK to be positioned like those already on the right side of the equation.

Keep reading.

It's time to make the system work FOR you and not AGAINST you like everyone else.

* * *

I looked up at Emile. He had just scribbled a whole bunch of things on this napkin, and I knew immediately I was hearing something special, but I had a million questions.

The expensive pen in his hand was clearly "experienced" from writing many of Emile's powerful concepts and ideas on paper.

I looked over to my mentor and then Emile the grandson.

They were all smiling.

I smiled. "This is great. In fact, it is amazing. But how do we shift over to the right side of the Wealth Equation?" I asked.

Emile flipped over the page to a new blank one, placed his pen on it, leaned back in his chair, and asked me a question.

Chapter Summary

- Understanding the Wealth Equation, known simply as WealthQ is the first step to building your wealth on auto-pilot.
- The second step is to understand that you need to move over to the "Receiving" side of the WealthQ.
- By moving over, you allow the four main forces of inflation, interest, taxes and opportunity cost to work for you instead of against you. There are actually more forces, but we only focus on these four in this book.
- The WealthQ Method is not about increasing returns or buying bigger assets, it is about a complete change in perspective on wealth building. It is about making the financial system work for you.

Chapter Three

The Traditional Method of Investing Doesn't Work!

"Tell me what you were taught in school and what you learned from books about building wealth?" asked Emile as he crossed his arms. There was a serious look on his face.

"Ummm. I'm not sure what you mean, but basically I was taught to save a certain amount of money every month and put it into a savings account. Then I should just let compounding take its course. That is wealth building in a nutshell, it is what it is" I said unsure of what he was really asking.

"Precisely. What else?"

"Be debt free and avoid any and all debt whatsoever."

"That's exactly true. That's what the majority teaches and unfortunately what the majority learns" he replied.

"Focus on getting a good return" I continued.

"Yep" he interrupted, "Now, before I go through how to move over to the right side of the Wealth Equation, there is a critical foundation piece you need to understand. In your mind I want you to turn over everything you have been told or read about wealth *building. Flip it on its head and then you will be able to build wealth!"* *he continued.*

"What do you mean?" I asked.

Emile then went on to completely turn everything I believed about building wealth on its head. And my mentor who sat next to me could only smile because he already understood.

* * *

The title of this chapter is a very bold one. But sadly, it's true, and it's true for most people. The traditional method of investing doesn't work. Most people work hard all their lives and use the traditional methods of investing their hard-earned money but never become wealthy because of their limited knowledge! Unfortunately, they will blame themselves thinking they didn't work hard enough or save enough, how sad!

The truth is they just lacked the information in this book!

Before I continue, I want you to know my assumptions about the people reading this book. These are the people I am trying to educate:

- I'm talking about people who are trying to build wealth from their INVESTMENTS, and not those trying to build wealth from entrepreneurship or an extremely high salary.
- I'm talking about people who invest the way many "experts" out there recommend, i.e. investing in the stock market, buying bonds, loading up their 401K, and buying real estate without using leverage.
- I'm talking about people who have been conditioned that any form of debt is bad.

Let's see if we can benefit from a walk down memory lane. In planning to grow your wealth there are multiple factors, variables, influences, and alternatives you need to understand and consider. Following are 9 considerations:

1: Cash

Let's start our journey with a fixed sum of money, say $10,000 in CASH.

You know the $10,000 won't build wealth sitting there in cash under your mattress. You need to make it work for you.

You decide to consider investing it.

2: The Compounding Environment

Let's review a lesson we all were taught many years ago in a class called mathematics. Your teacher shared this wonderful strategy about COMPOUNDING.

She said if you place your money in a compounding account, it will grow to a gazillion dollars after a gazillion years. You were so excited, you wanted that gazillion dollars.

In fact, your teacher shared that Albert Einstein once said "compound interest is the most powerful force in the universe". Now you knew how you would become rich!

She went on to ask this question to drive home the point:

"If I were to offer you one penny that I will double every day for thirty days or offer to give you $100,000 today, which would you choose?"

I remember we all guessed $100,000 just to find out we were wrong. She said a penny doubled every-day for thirty days would yield $5,368,709.12!

Wow! We were all astonished with our eyes bulging out!

But we weren't told about taxes at that time. So let's add taxes.

3: Tax Environment

Let's run the above penny doubling scenario in 3 different tax environments:

- Tax-Free Compounding Growth
- Tax-Deferred Compounding Growth
- Taxable Compounding Growth

TAX-FREE COMPOUNDING GROWTH	
Day	Growth
1	$ 0.01
2	$ 0.02
3	$ 0.04
4	$ 0.08
5	$ 0.16
...	...
28	$ 1,342,177.28
29	$ 2,684,354.56
30	**$ 5,368,709.12**

TABLE 5: **Tax-Free Growth for Penny Doubled Example**

TAX-DEFERRED COMPOUNDING GROWTH
30% TAX BRACKET

Day	Growth
1	$ 0.01
2	$ 0.02
3	$ 0.04
4	$ 0.08
5	$ 0.16
...	...
28	$ 1,342,177.28
29	$ 2,684,354.56
30	$ 3,758,096.38

Table 6: Tax-Deferred Growth for Penny Doubled Example

TAXABLE COMPOUNDING GROWTH
30% TAX BRACKET

Day	Growth
1	$ 0.01
2	$ 0.02
3	$ 0.03
4	$ 0.05
5	$ 0.08
...	...
28	$ 16,677.11
29	$ 28,351.09
30	$ 48,196.86

Table 7: Taxable Compounding Growth for Penny Doubled Example

Here are the results:

- Tax-Free Compounding Growth:
  - Penny turns into $5,368,709.12.
- Tax-Deferred Compounding Growth:
  - Penny turns into $3,758,096.38 (assuming 30% bracket).
- Taxable Compounding Growth:
  - Penny turns into $48,196.86 (assuming 30% bracket).

Whoa! Wait a minute! That $100,000 suddenly became attractive when compared to the last example!

You can clearly see how important understanding the tax environment is.

You decide to invest and use one of the tax-advantaged environments (tax-free or tax-deferred).

You are excited about having this "greatest force" working for you in the right tax environment.

After a few years, you review your growth, and realize something is off. You are not where you wanted and needed to be financially. What is going on?

Upon further investigation, you realize that you were being charged "low" fees that were connected to your investment.

4: Fees

"But the fees are low" you might think.

Let's look into an interview on PBS (public television) with John Bogle, the founder of Vanguard, one of the world's largest mutual fund organizations. John Bogle is one of the most respected names on Wall Street. (Refer to Resources page for the link to the interview.)

That interview opened my eyes.

It's sad that most people work a lifetime and invest their money into investments like mutual funds only to find out at their retirement date that they have been "had"… while the whole time, people like John Bogle had been warning them about what was happening!

Not benefitting from the available information is typical of the people on the "Paying" side of the WealthQ.

But now, back to John Bogle's interview.

In the interview, Mr. Bogle was asked *"So if my investment in your fund does your average, what percentage of my net growth is going to fees in a 401(k) plan?"*

To which Mr. Bogle replied:

"Well, it's awesome. Let me give you a little longer-term example. The example I use in my book is an individual who is 20 years old today starting to accumulate for retirement. That person has about 45 years to go before retirement -- 20 to 65 -- and then, if you believe the actuarial tables, another 20 years to go before death mercifully brings his or her life to a close. So that's 65 years of investing. If that individual invests $1,000 at the beginning of that time and earns 8%, their $1,000 will grow in that 65-year period to around $140,000.

Now, the financial system -- the mutual fund system in this case — will take about two and one half percentage points out of that return, so you will have a gross return of 8%, a net return of 5.5%, and your $1,000 will grow to approximately $30,000. One hundred ten thousand dollars goes to the financial system and $30,000 to you, the investor. Think about that. <u>That means the financial system put up zero percent of the capital and took zero percent of the risk and got almost 80% of the return, and you, the investor in this long time period, an investment lifetime, put up 100 percent of the capital, took 100% of the risk, and got only a little bit over 20% of the return.</u> That is a financial system that is failing investors because of those costs of financial advice and brokerage, some hidden, some out in plain sight that investors face today. So the system has to be fixed."

"Why didn't I know about this years ago?" You are thinking to yourself.

Do you have any idea how much of an impact your fees have on your investments?

So you decide to rework your investments to have minimal fees.

You will now be on your way you think.

But you would be wrong. The GREATEST FORCES would still be working against you.

Then comes inflation…

5: Inflation

Inflation? What does inflation have to do with your investments?

Besides, inflation is low. How does it affect you?

You say to yourself; "I am debt-free, own my assets free-and-clear, and my returns are good. I am being told I shouldn't worry about inflation—by those experts on TV".

Think again…not worrying about inflation turns out to be your biggest threat: your loss of purchasing power.

According to FOOL.COM, a well-respected website for stock news and analysis, *"Put simply, inflation slowly but surely saps the value of your hard-earned money. Even at a relatively low 3% inflation rate, prices double roughly every 25 years. Moreover, depending on your individual needs, your personal inflation rate might be much higher than the official Consumer Price Index. For instance, many retirees have argued that the CPI doesn't reflect their particular spending patterns, making it necessary to determine their own price-increase exposure and make arrangements accordingly.*

<u>*The steady erosion of purchasing power is the biggest reason why investing too conservatively can be problematic. If you keep money in a savings account right now, you guarantee that your account balance will never go down. But earning just a fraction of a percent in interest, you'll never keep up with even the low inflation rate that we've enjoyed lately"*</u>

So what is the inflation rate? You just might want to take a look at ShadowStats.com. You also just might want to be seated when you do.

According to ShadowStats.com, inflation is closer to 10% than the 3% that the government states. That's because the Consumer

Price Index or CPI (the index that measures inflation) was updated during the President Carter and President Clinton years, and energy (gas) and food were removed from the CPI, which in turn lowered the inflation rate. In plain English, they removed the food and gas we need to survive from the calculation for inflation! Huh? Yep, it's true.

Fortunately, ShadowStats.com keeps track of inflation using the old calculation.

So if inflation is indeed closer to 10%, and inflation <u>compounds</u>. What does that mean to you?

Simple.

Your investment of $10,000 has to return 10% after taxes and after fees, every single year, just to <u>maintain</u> its purchasing power, and your investment has to be growing in a compounding manner!

Where can you find such an investment?

If you are not sure then maybe you should consider:

- Real Estate? No, you were told by the experts on TV that having a mortgage is bad.

- Stock Market? According to the Dalbar Study, the average investor had an average return of just over 3% in the last 25 years. Dalbar Inc. is the nation's leading financial services, market research firm performing a variety of evaluations and ratings of practices and communications. Dalbar Inc. is committed to raising the standards of excellence in the financial services and healthcare industries. In other words, they are the ones to listen to.

- Bonds? Not even close.

- Mutual Funds? What a joke!

So you speak to another expert about what to do and what he said brings up another new variable to consider.

6: Opportunity Cost

This expert said that the largest cost for the average American is Opportunity Cost.

According to InvestorWords.com, Opportunity Cost is *"The cost of passing up the next best choice when making a decision. For example, if an asset such as capital is used for one purpose, the opportunity cost is the value of the next best purpose that capital could have been used for. Opportunity cost analysis is an important part of a company's decision-making processes, but is not treated as an actual cost in any financial statement."*

When you "park" your money in an account that grows in a compounding manner, you are losing the opportunity to make more money with that money. In fact, it is your biggest cost, bigger than any other cost.

Imagine putting $250 per month in an account "because the experts on television advised you to do that." That money could have made you a lot more money if you had used it right.

At this point, most people are puzzled.

What else can you do with it?

7: The Break-Even Return Equation

Here is a formula that makes all this real!

But, let's recap where we are first.

We had $10,000 cash, we used compounding (the "greatest force in the universe") on it, and that wasn't enough. We placed it in the right tax environment. That wasn't enough. We minimized fees. That wasn't enough. We considered inflation. We realized there is very little to nothing that can beat all the above including inflation. But even if there is, it has to beat it every year consistently! Let's go on.

This "Break-Even Return" is the return on investment you require to break even, before taxes, before inflation and after fees just to maintain purchasing power!

Here is the actual formula to calculate the break-even return you need:

R = Effective Tax Rate (federal & state)

I = Inflation Rate

B = Break-Even Rate

$$B = I / (1 - R)$$

Download a complimentary calculator to further help understand this concept. Refer to the Resources section in the back of this book for more information.

Again, this calculation shows you what you need to make as a return on your investment to break even before taxes, before inflation and after fees. This assumes the investment also offers compounding growth!

Let's plug in some numbers.

Let's use 40% for an effective tax rate, which includes state and federal taxes. Let's use 10% for inflation (according to ShadowStats.com). If you don't agree with 10% you should consider that all experts predict that inflation WILL be going up given all the money that is being printed right now.

$$B = I / (1 - R)$$
$$B = 10\% / (1 - 40\%)$$
$$B = 16.67\%$$

That means you need to receive a return of 16.67% from your investment to break even. Remember, this is before taxes, before inflation and after fees. This also assumes the investment offers compounding growth. Even more of a challenge this growth has to be a consistent return every year.

All that just to break even! Not to increase your wealth!

This is pretty bad.

Hopefully, you are beginning to see that the traditional method of investing doesn't work!

So, how is anyone building wealth then?

8: Balanced Portfolio

After doing all the right things above, you are then advised to have a "balanced" portfolio. A "balanced" portfolio you are told depends on many factors.

If your break-even rate was 16.67% as in our example, and you diversify half of your portfolio into "safer" assets such as bonds yielding 2%, that means the other half of your portfolio has to generate a crazy impossible return year after year in a compounding manner just to break even, not to build any wealth!

Are you kidding me?

For that to happen, that means you have to invest in higher volatile (higher risk) assets and pray you hit your numbers—just to break even!

It should be becoming abundantly clear that the traditional method of investing is broken, but still very few experts will admit it!

At this point, you might be thinking "but inflation is not 10%" therefore your numbers are off. I want you to consider two things. First, visit ShadowStats.com and do your own research. If it makes you feel better go ahead and plug in 6% or 7% for inflation. The numbers still don't make sense. Furthermore, you need to calculate your "personal inflation rate." We each have our own personal inflation rate depending on the things we purchase. Your personal inflation rate could differ dramatically from the national inflation rate. Calculating this figure can be eye-opening—unless of course you ride your bicycle to work and don't need to buy gas, and fast for weeks at a time!

The traditional method of investing doesn't work!

9: Financial Leverage

Finally, here it is, THE TRUTH: there is no way to build real wealth except to use LEVERAGE. Without leverage, it is virtually impossible to build wealth. Most "experts" on TV tell you not to use leverage, yet the affluent tell us they cannot do without it. You can see they are right. Their numbers prove it—and their wealth proves it as well.

Financial leverage can be good or it can be bad. It can work for you or it can destroy you financially.

However, once you know how to use it properly and manage the risk, it can MOVE you to the right side of the WealthQ.

The secret to moving to the "Receiving" side of the WealthQ is well-structured leverage!

What does leverage do?

Used right, leverage can move you to the right side of the Wealth Equation. Leverage allows you to position yourself on the receiving end of inflation. That means as inflation rises, you benefit. And, as you will find out leverage also positions you on the receiving end of interest and opportunity cost as well.

Leverage is to the wealthy as candy is to kids.

Here is an analogy I like for leverage.

Going back to our $10,000, instead of having just one $10,000 growing in a compounding environment and in a tax-advantaged environment, you can first "replicate" the $10,000 four times, and place each of those new $10,000 in a tax-advantaged compounding environment. Now you are working with $50,000 to start. Of course these amounts would be larger for the individuals that know how to use leverage effectively!

One of the keys to financial leverage is to have it structured correctly. We will expand on this later in the book.

> **This is not just any leverage. The key with this leverage is that it is correctly structured leverage. "Correctly structured" includes both the terms and the amount of leverage.**

When used properly you should think of financial leverage, as a REPLICATING process.

Now, let's put everything together.

We started with $10,000 cash. Now (using leverage) we will replicate it several times. So we have expanded the $10,000 to $50,000 instantly in this example. No waiting for a gazillion years! We now place each $10,000 into a compounding environment. We then make sure we place each of those five $10,000 sets in a tax advantaged environment. We make sure we minimize or eliminate fees. Then, because we are using leverage, inflation works to our advantage, as we will discover later in the book. Each $10,000 can return less than the 16.67% return we calculated earlier as "necessary", but the sum of all the $10,000 investments should easily beat that targeted return. Thus showing us we are actually building wealth.

In fact, as you will learn later in the book that $10,000 being used in this example can be "replicated" a lot more than just 5 times!

The important point to understand is that it is <u>the leverage</u> that is the key to making this work.

We like our new term for extremely successful investors who know how to use leverage: DEBT MILLIONAIRES.

A "Debt Millionaire"…

- Is someone who knows how to MANAGE debt to move themselves closer to their financial goals
- Uses debt STRATEGICALLY to build wealth
- Is one of the most sophisticated investors on the planet
- Is someone that understands that debt can destroy them if they don't manage it well

"Debt Millionaires" are the investors who know how to use debt strategically to move to the "Receiving" side of the WealthQ. They understand "The WealthQ Method" of investing.

As a reminder, most people follow the "experts" on television who are saying that debt and leverage are bad. However, in this book, for you the reader we will continue talking about debt and leverage. From here forward you will come to understand the importance of using debt and learning about and using leverage.

The good news is, the best part of what you will learn has not yet been revealed! We are just starting out.

* * *

I was intrigued by Emile's information, but I was not convinced. I wanted more information.

The waiter then interrupted us. "Gentlemen, are you ready to order?"

"The usual for me" said Emile as he looked at me "Remember this. No one in this universe cares more about your finances than you. Take the time to learn about finance. What I will share with you will change the way you look at investing forever."

Chapter Summary

When investing there are multiple factors, variables, influences, and alternatives to be considered. We looked at and discussed:

- 1: We started with some cash, then
- 2: We put it into a compounding environment, then
- 3: We made sure we placed everything in a tax-advantaged environment, then
- 4: We made sure we minimized or eliminated fees, then
- 5: We considered how inflation affects our investments, then
- 6: We made sure we considered the opportunity cost, then
- 7: We calculated the actual "Break Even Return" we need before taxes and inflation, and after fees. The break-even return needed just to break even and not even build wealth was high!, then
- 8: We added "balanced" portfolio. That translated to our having to invest in much higher risk assets just to break even!, then
- 9: We learned how financial leverage will allow us to replicate the above several times to speed up our wealth, and in fact allow us to BECOME wealthy.
- The traditional method of investing doesn't work!
- "Debt Millionaires" are the ones who know how to use debt strategically to move to the "Receiving" side of WealthQ. They understand "The WealthQ Method" of investing.
- Use leverage properly and you can become a "Debt Millionaire."

Chapter Four

Hacking the System

Emile grabbed his pen to write a note on his pad, but then he paused. He was deep in thought. He was trying to say something.

I could tell he was being very patient with me trying to take me along on this journey of moving me from the "Paying" side to the "Receiving" side.

"Before jumping into the details of the Wealth Equation, you need to understand the big picture—the game of finance. You need to understand the game, and in doing so, you will appreciate how to use the system and make it work for you…"

"Let's consider a simple example George" he said as he moved pen to paper.

* * *

When playing the game of finance, you need to understand it well enough to be able to find ways to win.

I occasionally use the term "hacking the game of finance" and I mean just that. I am not talking about doing anything illegal but simply finding shortcuts to make the system work for you instead of against you.

To "hack the game of finance", you need three steps:

1. You need to understand who created the system, because there-in lies the biggest clues. "They" have built the system to work for them. In this book the "They" we are talking about are the global bankers.

2. You need to understand how the system works. We will not be doing that in this book, but rather we will be giving you an indication of how the WealthQ was discovered and why "The WealthQ Method" is so effective.

3. You need to recognize that many of our beliefs about money, investing and the financial system were actually initiated by the ones that created the financial system. They did this in order to make us function better inside their system. Instructions and beliefs like "pick a 15-year mortgage over a 30-year mortgage" actually benefit them and not us (refer to my book *The Wealthy Code*). It is important that you question all your financial beliefs and what were the true intentions behind those beliefs.

Once you have addressed and worked through these three steps, then the fun starts. Remember, it's a game that you play. With your new understanding of the answers to the three steps many things are possible including playing the game to win.

In order to understand step 1 above, here is another analogy. As kids, we all played with Legos. We all built homes and various other structures. We started with a green base plate (now they have other colors) and used it as the foundation on which we built a structure; let's use a house as an example. Refer to the following diagram.

FIGURE 1: INVESTORS FOCUS ON WHAT'S ON THE BASE PLATE, BUT NEVER THINK ABOUT THE BASE PLATE ITSELF.

We were all focused on the house, how it looked, the garage with a car, the people pieces etc. But what happened if we accidently dropped the base plate on the floor? Everything on it, including the cars, the structures, and the people were all destroyed. But when we were building the house we never thought about that base plate, which was the underlying foundation of everything.

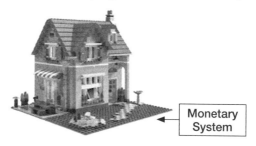

FIGURE 2: THE BASE PLATE REPRESENTS THE MONETARY SYSTEM UPON WHICH EVERYTHING IS BUILT ON.

That is exactly what happens in real life. That base plate represents the monetary system on which everything is built. Investors are so focused on their real estate, or their businesses, or their investments, they take the base plate for granted, yet it is the foundation underlying their investments. The more you know about how that foundation is built, the better you can build on it. In fact, the base plate actually represents multiple "layers", the monetary system is one layer and the economy is a layer on top of the monetary system.

Again, these multiple layers are beyond the scope of this book, but it is good for you to know they are there. This book will focus on how to "build" your investments on the monetary base. The WealthQ Method was built to work WITH the monetary system that is the base. That is why it is so effective.

Here is a simple example to illustrate this.

You were always told the way you become rich is to save a certain amount of money every month into an interest bearing account. For example, save $200 every month into a savings account, and then use that money to purchase the saved for products and services.

You should never incur any debt whatsoever, and if you do have any debt, you should pay it off!

The more you understand the financial system, the easier it is to analyze the challenges with the above example. Our financial system is based on debt, and therefore inflation happens! Other things happen too.

The banks want your money, so they convince you to deposit it with them. You allow it to sit there idle while it supposedly grows, meanwhile they are using your money to skyrocket their own wealth. You even fell for the belief that compound interest in THEIR bank was good. But let's keep going with this example.

You are placing $200 per month into an account earning 1% to 3% depending on the account (if you are lucky).

1. The measly little bit of interest you are earning on that account is being taxed. So your return is much less than the stated interest amount. **So taxes work to your disadvantage in this scenario.**

2. Inflation is much higher than the after-tax return you are receiving, which means you are losing purchasing power of that $200. In plain English, it means over time, you can buy less goods and services with that $200! That will be covered in more detail in chapter seven. **So inflation also works to your disadvantage in this scenario.**

3. Your $200 is sitting there doing nothing, so you are losing the opportunity to do something with it. This is called "lost opportunity cost." This will be covered in more detail in chapter six. **So opportunity cost also works to your disadvantage in this scenario.**

I only picked three things to analyze. In all three situations the system forces are working against you—inflation, opportunity cost, and taxes.

As you can see, the model of saving a certain amount of money in a "safe" account is doing you no good. You are "losing" in many ways because of how the base plate (the monetary system) was built.

But the teacher's calculator showed we would end up with a gazillion dollars in a gazillion years! You now know that was their conditioning of you to see numbers that didn't reflect "real" dollars as you will find out later in chapter seven on inflation.

So let's go back now and "flip" what you know on its head.

You know that the bankers have their system set up for you to use but to make them richer, not you. One of the ways they squeeze money out of you is with inflation among other things. One "hack" we use is debt as was mentioned before to counter these "forces" that were created. Debt is actually more than just a hack, it is a weapon. Debt as a hack works because of the way the base plate, the (monetary system) was built.

Before we dive into debt, first let's talk about what is "good debt" and what is "bad debt." "Good debt" is debt that we use to purchase assets that appreciate or pay us regularly, or both. "Bad debt" is consumer debt that takes money from our pocket, such as credit cards, auto loans, etc. In this book, all debt we talk about is good debt, but more importantly, good debt that is structured correctly, because "good debt" can hurt us if structured incorrectly. Currently, most investors seem to structure their so-called "good debt" incorrectly. More on this later.

Now, let's get INTO debt, specifically, "good debt." This simplistic example is here to illustrate a point. Later in the book, we will expand it a lot and improve it.

Let's say you purchased a $100k asset with 6%-interest debt, and let's assume you decided to pay the debt down with the $200 per month you were going to "save" up.

You don't do this for the sake of buying an asset, but rather to get into well-structured debt. This statement will become obvious later. For now, notice how I said that. You buy the asset to get into debt, not the other way around. I will expand on that later.

So here are some of the characteristics of your loan:

- By using the $200 per month to pay against the loan, you are essentially "saving" 6% (in this example), which is similar to making 6% tax-free. **So taxes work to our advantage—i.e. we are not paying taxes on "saved" money.** As a reminder, previously, you were depositing the $200 into an account, being paid a lot less than 6%, and paying taxes on that measly interest rate.

- By using debt, you are using other people's money to buy the asset, and not our money. That means you are not losing the opportunity of buying the asset in the future for all cash, you are buying it today. **So you are gaining the advantage of the opportunity, and that works to your advantage.**

- Since you are using debt to buy the asset today, and you are paying for it over time, you are using the "time value of money" to your advantage. That essentially means you are paying for it with future money. The $200 payments are spread out over many years which means it is "cheaper" money. This allows you to use inflation to your advantage. In other words, **inflation works to your advantage!** More on this later.

We use our understanding of the financial system to turn things around. By using this understanding we are not playing against the creators of the financial system. Using the right tools, you are now aligned with the creators of the financial system and the system now works for you, not against you. You are not "partnering" with them, you are simply hacking the game of finance that they created to improve your lifestyle. The result is that your net-worth skyrockets over time from the simple example above—automatically.

That is how you play the game.

That is how WealthQ was discovered.

So what is the most important strategy to move you from the "Paying" side to the "Receiving" side of the Wealth Equation? It is debt. But only the right type of correctly structured debt.

It is DEBT that allows you to move from the "Paying" side of the Wealth Equation to the "Receiving" side, but only the right type of correctly structured debt.

However, you know debt can also hurt you. Debt is a double edged-sword. Sophisticated investors, called "Debt Millionaires" know how to measure, control, and manage debt, and use it to build wealth and move them to the right side of the WealthQ.

We will cover some of these strategies later in the book.

* * *

Emile had explained how the financial system works, how interest really works, how big bankers use inflation to work to their advantage and not for the average consumer, how taxes are really just interest payments, the monetary system, and also addressed many other things.

It all started to make sense to me.

But it seemed overwhelming.

He kept assuring me that anyone can play this game of finance and win by simply understanding the game.

The banking financial structure started to remind me of the movie "The Matrix." We are all pawns in this game of finance, but once our eyes are opened, we can indeed use the available tools and knowledge to make the system work for us. Understanding the WealthQ was the key.

Chapter Summary

- We are all players in the game of finance. To play the game better, it's important to understand WHO created the game (the financial system), and then HOW the system works, which includes the monetary system etc. Finally we must question everything we have been told about money and investing because these beliefs were spread to serve the creators of the system.
- The secret to moving from the "Paying" side to the "Receiving" side of the WealthQ is DEBT. It has to be the right type of correctly structured debt.
- The three new terms we have introduced are:
    - The Wealth Equation (aka. WealthQ) which has 2 sides in the equation; the "Paying" side and the "Receiving" side.
    - The WealthQ Method is the method of investing that focuses on moving the investor to the right side of the WealthQ.
    - The Debt Millionaires are those investors who have implemented "The WealthQ Method" and have mastered the use of debt to move to the right side of the WealthQ.

Section Two

The Wealth Equation

Chapter Five

Moving to the Receiving Side of Interest

"But is it that bad to be on the left side of the WealthQ" I asked everyone. "I mean, how bad is it?"

The silence was deafening.

My mentor looked at me and then uttered these words "The people on the left side are slaves to the system! They will spend their entire lives being slaves to the system, and what's worse they will never know it!"

"Slaves to the system"—those words kept resonating in my mind. They were very powerful, image provoking words.

"Okay" I said. "I understand that I need to move to the right side. I now understand that debt is the key to moving to the right side. How do I tackle each of those forces you mentioned?"

"Let's start with interest first, It's the easiest to grasp" said Emile.

* * *

Albert Einstein said, 'Those who understand interest, earn it, those who don't, pay it.'

There is so much significant meaning in that statement, a lot more than most people realize. Let's dive in.

The Problem with Interest

Imagine a world with only two people, Bob and Carl.

Bob has $1,000, and that represents all the money in their world.

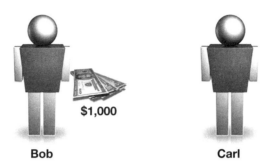

**FIGURE 3: BOB AND CARL—
$1,000 REPRESENTS ALL THE MONEY IN THEIR WORLD**

Carl needs $500. So he borrows it from Bob at 10%. Carl agrees to pay Bob back $550 (principal and interest).

Sometime later, Carl pays back $500 of the $550. Bob now has his $1,000 back, and is awaiting his remaining $50 in interest. But the $1,000 represents all the money in their world. From where would Carl obtain the remaining $50?

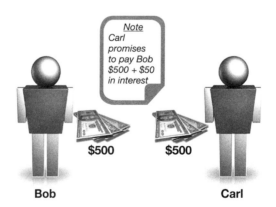

**FIGURE 4: CARL BORROWED $500 AT 10% FROM BOB.
CARL NOW OWES BOB $500 IN PRINCIPAL AND $50 IN INTEREST (ANNUALLY)**

Carl can do one of two things: Carl can work for Bob for $50 in lieu of paying him the $50, or Carl can borrow the money from Bob to pay Bob back.

Let's consider the latter. Carl borrows another $500 at 10% interest. He agrees to pay Bob $550 (principal and interest), in addition to the original $50, in unpaid interest. Carl now owes Bob a total of $600.

Sometime later, Carl pays Bob the second $500, and now has $100 of unpaid interest still to pay. However, Bob now has the whole $1,000 that exists in their world. Carl has no way of paying Bob the remaining $100. Once again, he has two choices—work for Bob or borrow more money.

By now, I hope you see that as long as Carl keeps borrowing money from Bob, he will owe more and more over time until the point where he will have to work for Bob at some point.

There actually is a third option. Carl could file bankruptcy.

The point of this story is that as long as someone charges interest, this "created" money does not really exist. Therefore, ultimately, someone will have to work for it, or keep borrowing money until they work for it, or at some point, file bankruptcy.

There actually is another choice. If Carl worked for Bob, and Bob paid Carl enough to make his payments, Carl could keep working for Bob until Bob was paid off. So, eventually, Carl will be obligated to work for Bob or declare bankruptcy.

On a side note, if you are paying interest right now, we need to change that. But back to that a little later. Let's continue with our flow.

One can argue that someone could borrow the money, create something of value, such as bake some bread, and profit from it. That is true, so let's expand on that.

In the next diagram, we have a banker lending money to a producer (baker in our example) to produce a product (bread in our example).

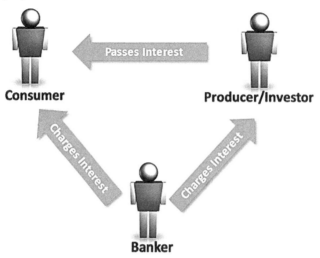

FIGURE 5: THREE TEAMS IN THIS WORLD

The producer produces the product and sells it to the consumer. Note that the interest charged by the banker is being passed along to the ultimate consumer of the product. That means the consumer ultimately pays the interest. Note they (the producer and the consumer) have to work hard to pay that "created" money.

Look at this transaction again, I recommend that you think this all the way through. It is <u>not</u> easy. But at the core of it, we end up with the three teams: consumer, producer and banker.

The consumer borrows money from the banker and pays interest.

The producer borrows money from the banker, creates a product or service, and passes the interest to the consumer, which ultimately means the consumer pays for the interest along with profits to the producer.

Yes, there is value to the consumer. But let's focus on the money flow here.

Ultimately, the consumer pays in every scenario, by paying the banker directly (think about your credit cards for example), or indirectly through the producer by buying a product where the producer passed on the interest that the banker charged the producer. When you look at the system it is no surprise that with many couples, both have to work and are still barely making it. I hope this is starting to make clear for you why 34.5% of the average American's take-home income goes to financial institutions to cover the interest alone—they are working for the banker!

You might be wondering why I have "Investor" near producer in the previous diagram. Investors do a similar thing that producers do. For example, with real estate investors, their "product" just happens to be rental properties. They need to sell a valuable product to the consumer for the consumer to "buy" this product. The real estate investor is doing just that. They borrow from the banker (a mortgage) to buy their rental property, and then rent out that property to the consumer, and pass the interest payment on the mortgage to the consumer through the rent.

Now, that might seem unfair that the consumer ends up paying for interest from both sides, directly to the banker and indirectly through the producer. Well, there are several ways to look at this. At the end of the day, the consumer is receiving something of value, and they are willing to work for it. There is nothing wrong with that.

Lenders <u>create</u> new money that doesn't exist with interest. Someone has to borrow more money or work to pay the interest off.

So, what's the point of all of this? It's quite simple.

There are 3 teams in this world, consumers, producers and bankers.

Consumers pay interest, and they end up being the slaves to the system—working to pay off "created" money that doesn't exist!

Going back to what Albert Einstein said, 'Those who understand interest earn it, those who don't, pay it.' He was really saying that you can be on one of two sides, the master or the slave depending on if you are earning it or paying it. Those who understand interest and what it does, position themselves on the earning side (masters), otherwise, you are automatically on the other side, a slave to the financial system. Unfortunately many people have lifelong journeys of paying debt.

To be on the "Receiving" side of interest, you can be either the banker or the producer. You can either create interest or pass it on and make money off of it. This will be explained in more detail a little later.

To be on the "Receiving" side of interest in the WealthQ, you can either CREATE interest or PASS it on to the others.

Most of the population is on the "Paying" side of interest. This includes interest on mortgages, car loans, student loans, furniture loans, credit cards and a host of other things. In fact, it is believed that the average American spends 34.5% of their take home income on interest, not principal and interest, but rather interest alone over their lifetime.

The world is divided into three teams: the consumer, the producer and the banker.

Bankers and producers are also consumers, but they are bankers or producers first; consumers second.

Every person on this planet is in one of these three teams. There is no other choice. By default, people start as consumers. The rich are producers and bankers.

What most people don't realize is they can also be on the "bankers" team, as explained in my previous book *The Banker's Code*.

Imagine Jack goes shopping at his favorite retail store. He ends up buying $500 worth of goods. He uses his credit card. By doing so, here is what happened behind the scenes.

- Jack paid the banker in two ways—he paid the banker interest directly on the credit card. Then he paid indirectly because of the producers who passed the interest on their loans from the bankers into and as a part of the cost of the goods in the $500 purchase.
- Jack also paid a profit to the producer on the purchase.

Jack, the consumer, is needed to drive the economy. He is on the "Paying" side of interest. The banker was on the "Receiving" side, and so was the producer, creating an "arbitrage" situation—borrowing money from the banker and passing the interest cost on to Jack the consumer and then keeping the profit.

Also, as mentioned in my previous book, *The Bankers Code*, any individual can become a lender. In fact, with the boom in peer-to-peer lending (and crowd funding), even more so now, anyone can become a lender.

But there is more to it than that

Here is a caveat though which may seem counter intuitive. Lending might be good for interest, but lending can also be very bad for inflation! So it's not that simple.

When banks lend money for 30 years for a low interest rate, inflation works to their disadvantage. Lending $100,000 today and receiving payments for the next 30 years, the value of the payments in the future is not the same as today.

So if a banker does offer that 30-year loan, they then move to the "Receiving" side of interest, but they also move to the "Paying" side of inflation. Read that again, and carefully.

This might seem like bankers are not doing the right thing. But bankers don't really do exactly that as we shall find out.

So how does one move to the "Receiving" side of interest without giving up the inflation position?

There are several ways:

1. Lend money at an interest rate that is higher than the inflation rate after taxes, especially if the loans are short term loans, 12 months or less for example.
2. Borrow money at a lower rate and lend it out or invest it at a higher rate.
3. Use the "velocity of money" to turn money around as it comes in to increase your overall yield.

This first point is covered in detail in my previous book; *The Banker's Code*. In that book I write about the need for private lenders and why many borrowers are willing to pay higher rates than the inflation rate to these private lenders and also why this can be a win-win situation for both parties.

Essentially, there are many borrowers out there that have access to great deals on various assets, and they are willing to pay a premium to acquire those assets at a discount. Doing this gives them ample room in the deal to "share" in the profit or to pay a higher interest rate in exchange for faster and easier access to money rather than through traditional banks.

Banks do not lend against distressed properties and therefore it is not uncommon to find borrowers who are able to purchase real estate properties at great discount and then pay 12% interest on a 1-year loan, thus allowing them to profit from acquisition and disposition of that property.

On websites such as LendingClub.com and Prosper.com, 7% to 11% rates are not un-common. These companies lend money to consumers at these rates allowing them to consolidate their much more expensive credit card debts.

For point #2, this is a common theme for investors and business owners (producers). They are basically borrowing money to purchase assets (income properties or businesses) at a low rate and investing the money into those income producing assets that will pay more. This procedure is well covered in my book *The Wealthy Code*. In doing so, these investors are passing the interest onto the end consumer.

For example, if an investor purchases a property that pays (rental income) more than the cost of money on the mortgage this allows the investor to make the spread or the difference. By doing so, they are passing on the interest to the renters of that property.

Similarly, many investors and business owners that use borrowed money are simply passing the interest onto the end consumer. Once again, this passing of the interest puts the banker or the investor/producer on the "Receiving" side of interest in the WealthQ.

In the normal course, the responsibility for paying interest ends up being on the consumer. The consumer pays the banker interest directly for using the borrowed money to buy products and services. Think about how a consumer uses a credit card to buy "stuff" from retail stores. Then the consumer also pays interest to the banker indirectly for the interest on the purchases of goods and services by the producers/investors.

Ask yourself this simple question. Are you paying rent right now and if so how much of your payment is interest on a mortgage payment by someone else (your landlord)? There may be lots of interest built into your rent payment.

In fact that is how banks use mortgage-backed securities. They are lending money to consumers and borrow the money at a lower rate from Wall Street by selling the loans as mortgage-backed securities.

So the bankers are playing a very interesting game. By lending money, they are on the "Receiving" side of interest. And by borrowing the money from Wall Street, they are shifting the inflation disadvantage mentioned above to the buyers of that security. In other words, the average consumer who ultimately purchased that security (mortgage-backed security) is now the one that is on the "PAYING" side of inflation, and the banker now remains on the "RECEIVING" side of interest and inflation!

Buying Everyday Things

We touched on the basics of arbitraging interest (passing interest), but what about every day interest to credit cards and other loans? After all, everyone needs to buy a car at some point or buy "stuff" on credit cards.

Well, this is where things become very interesting. Very wealthy families for years have been using a concept called The Family Bank to lend money to family members and to themselves. It's based on the concept that Mayer Rothschild developed with his family, and it has worked ever so well since the 1700's.

This concept is called The Family Bank and is discussed in more detail in chapter twelve. The Family Bank Game teaches you how to redirect the interest payments you are now paying right into your own financing "company." Thus your dependency on 3rd party lenders is less, and you are moving to the right side of interest. Again, chapter twelve will describe in more detail on how The Family Bank will move you to the right side of interest.

Passing Interest

When passing interest to a consumer or another person, it is important that you do it right.

Again, let's look at various examples of passing interest. You are borrowing money, paying interest to the lender, and somehow making more money on the borrowed money.

There are various metrics to look at when doing so. I cover that in more detail in my book *The Wealthy Code*. Here are the highlights from the book:

- The capitalization rate on the income stream (from the asset) should be larger than the annual loan constant and the interest rate on the loan, or more appropriately the cost of money (Refer to the chapter Debt Metrics).
- Match the loan period of the underlying loan with the exit strategy on the income stream. For example, if you are buying an income producing asset for ten years, make sure the underlying loan used to purchase the asset is a ten year or longer loan.

Download a complimentary calculator to further help understand this concept. Refer to the Resources section in the back of this book for more information.

These are some of the guidelines when passing interest. Again, read my book *The Wealthy Code* for more detailed information.

So What to Do?

We just covered different aspects of interest. Once you understand all the various "forces" mentioned including interest, inflation, taxes and opportunity cost, you will be able to better formulate how to tie everything together and make better decisions for your investments.

But for now, these are some important lessons you can use immediately from this chapter:

- Be a producer, investor or banker. Learn how to pass interest or create interest.
- Pay off all your high-interest consumer debt, especially credit cards. This allows you to move to the right side of interest.
- If you decide to "pass" interest, learn how to use debt effectively. Knowledge is the key.
- Consider building a Family Bank for your family. This is covered in chapter twelve.
- Be aware of the annual loan constant; the interest rate compared to the capitalization rate as mentioned in the previous section and in my book *The Wealthy Code*.
- Do not pay off your other low interest consumer loans (such as car loans) yet. Not until you have read chapter six on Opportunity Cost.

* * *

I was intrigued. I wanted to know about this "family bank" concept, but I pretended I knew. I would ask my mentor later, and he would explain it to me.

As for my credit cards, I had already created a plan to pay them off and was already on track.

I also owned a few rental properties where I was passing the interest to the tenants and making a profit off of it.

I was excited about moving to the "Receiving" side of interest.

Chapter Summary

- You are either paying interest, creating interest or passing interest. You want to be on the side of the latter two.
- One of the ways to recapture the interest you are paying out is to start your own financing entity called a family bank. That is covered in chapter 12.
- Examples include buying commercial properties, becoming a private money lender, and using your family bank.
- Redirect most consumer debts for now into your family bank, or pay them off, especially credit cards.
- When structuring deals to pass interest from lender to someone else, be aware of certain metrics such as period of loan, exit strategy, annual loan constant, interest rate, cost of money and capitalization rate. Refer to the appendix on debt metrics.
- Read the book *The Wealthy Code* on structuring debt.

Chapter Six

Moving to the Receiving Side of Opportunity Cost!

"Where do you deposit your pay checks or your rent checks when you receive them?" asked Emile.

"In the bank?" I answered hesitantly. *"Where else would I deposit them?"*

Was I missing something I wondered?

Emile smiled and asked *"Do you deposit them in your checking account?"*

"Umm. Yes. Where else?" I questioned.

I must be missing something!

"You are losing six to seven figures over your lifetime in opportunity cost" he declared.

"Wow!"

* * *

Consider this. Without changing your lifestyle, without adding an additional income stream, without giving up your lattes, and by simply understanding and using "opportunity cost" to your advantage you can increase your net-worth significantly!

On the other hand, not implementing this in your life could be a huge "leak" in your wealth bucket.

This is the power of "opportunity cost."

We have lived our lives with certain beliefs that have been passed down for generations. Things like "debt is bad", "live debt free", and "pay cash for everything" have become ingrained in our minds. People on the "Receiving" side of the WealthQ understand opportunity cost. Everything these people know goes against the beliefs the general public (those on the left side of the Wealth Equation) have been brought up on and taught to believe.

First, let's understand what opportunity cost means.

Every financial decision you make has missed opportunity potential. For example, if you made the decision to invest $20,000 into buying a car and not buying a stock, that is a missed opportunity. In fact, the cost of missed financial opportunities can be calculated.

For example, imagine that buying the car in the above example allowed you to own the car free and clear but the stock ended up being $45,000 in five years. You obviously missed out on that opportunity. You could have used a low-interest car loan to buy the car and invested your capital in buying the stock.

The ability to make better financial decisions about the use of money can result in a significant increase in your net worth. In fact, it's believed that the biggest cost to the average American, more than taxes and inflation, is opportunity cost.

It is believed that the biggest cost to the average American, more than taxes and inflation, is opportunity cost.

Many people think this is hypothetical. It is not. Lost opportunity costs are the actual money you lose due to financial decisions you make versus different financial decisions.

There are certain financial decisions made every day around the world that result in people losing six to seven figures over their lifetimes. Just from that one single decision! You will learn how and be able to calculate that number in this chapter.

So again, opportunity cost is the cost we "pay" when we give up something to obtain something else.

According to investopedia.com, the definition of opportunity cost is "The cost of an alternative that must be forgone in order to pursue a certain action. Put another way, the benefits you could have received by taking an alternative action."

Opportunity cost is the cost we pay when we give up something to obtain something else.

Now let's try to put a number to this by looking at a simple example.

Swanee has $10,000 to invest and has a choice between Stock A and Stock B, the opportunity cost is the difference in their returns. If she invested $10,000 in Stock A and received a 6% return while Stock B makes an 8% return, the opportunity cost is 2%.

Think of the opportunity cost as the additional amount of money one could have made by making a different investment decision.

Looking at the opportunity cost of each choice can help you find the most valuable opportunity. Learn how to calculate opportunity cost with these basic methods.

So, again, what does this mean to you, the reader? Understanding and implementing this could mean an additional SEVEN FIGURES or more in your net-worth over time!

That's the goal. Keep reading!

Opportunity cost as a topic can become quite complex. I will focus on a very narrow domain here to maximize your understanding of the topic, but actually, more importantly, your net-worth. I won't bore you with details, but I will give you the relevant information that you need.

Let's start with some basics.

Grab a dollar bill from your pocket right now.

Really, go ahead. Grab one.

Look at it carefully, and ask yourself this simple question—"What can you do with that dollar?"

1. You can buy something with it
2. You can invest it
3. You can put it back into your pocket

Now let's expand on each of these:

"You can buy something with it"—in this case, you give it to someone else for a product or service. You lose it. You also give up everything that dollar could have brought you if invested—such as returns, interest etc.

"You can invest it"—You give up the products & services you could have purchased in exchange for having interest or return being generated from the dollar.

"You can put it back into your pocket"—and end up doing one of the 2 options mentioned above at a future date. Moving forward, I will eliminate this option since it ends up being one of the 2 above, but it's indeed a 3rd option you should consider.

So let's say you decide to buy a coffee. You can spend the money and buy it, and give up the interest or return you could have earned on that money. The alternative is you can borrow money to buy that coffee and keep your money. This means you are now paying someone else interest on the borrowed money. This allows you to possibly use your money for investments etc.

So here are your 2 options.

FIGURE 6: TWO MAIN OPTIONS WHEN PURCHASING

For every purchase, you typically have 2 options to finance it: Either pay cash and give up the interest you would have received on that cash, or borrow money to purchase it and pay interest to someone else. In both cases, you are financing it.

By making the correct decisions on when to use *your money* or *borrowed money* for specific transactions can make such a huge difference in your net worth.

This introduces a very important aspect to using your money efficiently to maximize your use of your money—debt. Specifically, the using of debt strategically to maximize the return on your money.

You will notice a common thread to this book—the use of debt as a strategic tool to move to the "Receiving" side of the WealthQ.

So let's expand on this with an example mentioned earlier.

You can buy a car with your $20,000 and own it free and clear from loans. However, you could have used a car loan to buy it that would have cost you 3% interest over five years, and invested that $20,000 into an investment that paid you 6%.

If you financed the car at 3% and invested the money with a 6% return, you would have made a 3% (difference/spread) profit.

As investors, you have to understand opportunity cost, and recognize ways to choose the right financing option for the right acquisitions.

> **As investors, you have to understand opportunity cost, and recognize ways to choose the right financing option for the right acquisitions.**

Now, let's take this a step further.

Let's go through an example of lost opportunity cost to make a point.

You have $50,000 in your checking account and that's the only money you have designated for investing. Where is the BEST place to invest it for the best return?

Take a minute and think about it.

There is a 99.99% chance you are wrong, but keep thinking about it.

Well, it's not any of the investments you mentioned—unless you have heard me speak about this before.

The best place for the highest return is in your checking or savings account, or any other liquid account!

Here's why.

Let's assume you invested that $50,000 as down payment into purchasing a $250,000 rental property. That money now is locked up for some time, say five years or more. Let's assume your return is X%. However, that money is now locked up, and you have no liquid funds to invest, therefore your chances of obtaining another loan from a lender to purchase another asset have declined significantly (due to lack of liquidity).

On the other hand, if you kept that $50,000 in your liquid account and brought in an equity partner to put up the down payment for a piece of the upside, now you are a part owner of the property and you still have your $50,000.

You are able to replicate an equity partner transaction multiple times. Your money in the liquid account gives you a much better chance of obtaining more financing to purchase more assets. If you offered your equity partner 50% and they accepted then you could have multiple deals while holding on to your $50,000.

Holding that $50,000 in a liquid account gives you the opportunity to do many more loans, thereby significantly improving your returns from just that amount alone.

That is the difference between looking for a "return" and a "spread". When you invest your money, you are looking for a "return," but you lock up your money and lose the opportunity to make more money with it. Looking for a "spread" allows you to make more money using other people's money and you also have the ability to do many of them. So in essence, that $50,000 in your liquid account allows you to generate many more "spreads" than "returns."

Let's consider another example.

You deposit your paycheck in a bank. The money sits there until you pay your bills. Assume it takes you 3 weeks to pay off all your bills. That means your money sits there earning very little to nothing for up to 3 weeks out of every month (assuming you are paid once a month). So your money is doing nothing for 75% of the time you have it. If you work for 40 years, all the money you earn over the 40 years, up to 75% of the time is doing nothing for you sitting in a checking account waiting to pay bills. That is up to 30 years (75% of the 40 years) of money doing nothing! It is however, making the bank richer! What if you could make the money "earn" you 6% to 8% tax-free while sitting in the same bank you use? And it was still liquid? This is lost opportunity cost, and the difference is six to seven figures in your pocket without changing your lifestyle. And yes, that is possible!

These were just two examples of lost opportunity cost. There are a lot more, and it is costing you by you not doing something about it!

By the way, the last example mentioned is covered in *The Wealthy Code* book in more detail.

So let's add more to the two options from before.

We previously mentioned that you typically have 2 options to finance things: Either pay cash and give up the interest you would have received on that cash, or borrow money to purchase it and pay interest to someone else.

Now we can add another consideration.

How much more valuable is having cash than spending it? Another way of thinking about it is how much additional borrowed money can we access for having the cash?

So by having the $50,000 in our bank, does that allow us to have access to an additional $1,000,000 in loans, $2,000,000, or more? That depends on a number of factors. I hope you can see the magnitude of leverage you can generate with that liquidity.

How much more valuable is having cash than spending it? Another way of thinking about it is how much additional borrowed money can we access by having the cash?

So let's expand on this and cover another aspect of it. When we decide to use other people's money, what type should we use?

Note that I used the term "other people's money" here and not "debt" as I used earlier. The reason is that the use of other people's money can be structured in several ways other than just debt.

For example I can structure raised money as equity. For example I can pay a money partner a percentage of the income and/or profits from the investment in which they are involved. They invest their $50,000 into an investment and I can offer them 50% of the profit.

Another example is that I can structure the raised money as debt. For example, I can pay the investor investing their money a specific return on their loan.

Another example is that I can structure the raised money as royalty. For example, I can pay the investor investing their money a percentage of the gross income from the investment they are involved in. This is different than an equity partner since equity partner can have ownership.

There is also the option of structuring the deal as a combination of the above.

Furthermore, each of the above has various options to consider. For example, with debt, we have various types of debt including:

- Installment loans
- HELOC
- Mortgage
- Credit cards

Let's consider some specific examples to illustrate the above.

1. Instead of using your money for down payment on an asset, consider finding someone as an equity partner. An equity partner is someone that invests money in exchange for a percentage of the profit. The equity partner invests the down payment in exchange for piece of the profit. You could be on the loan and you keep your cash for liquidity.

2. Many investors that do short term deals (one year or less) tend to refinance to pull money out for these short term loans. It's actually better to have a HELOC instead of refinancing if the money is for funding these short term purchases.

3. Always keep your financials looking strong to be able to obtain financing for purchases. This includes your credit score, your debt-to-income ratio, liquidity, etc.

4. Consider having certain loans in your name and others under your partners' or spouses' name. Avoid both

of you being on the loan because it impacts your borrowing capacity.

5. Use 30-year mortgages over 15-year mortgages.
6. Find the lowest annual loan constant for all your loans for as long as possible. Refer to the book *The Wealthy Code* for more information.
7. Instead of using your credit card for large purchases, consider using your family bank. This is discussed later in the book. By doing this, you are recapturing higher interest payments and directing them into your pocket.

Calculating Opportunity Cost:

What about calculating lost opportunity cost? Well, this is where it gets interesting. The calculation depends on the underlying choices, but many times, for investing, you can use the "Future Value" formula to do so.

Here is the formula:

$$FV = PV (1 + r)^n$$

FV = Future Value

PV = Present Value

r = Rate (keep it simple, use annual rate)

n = number of periods (keep it simple, use number of years)

This formula will give you the value in the future of an investment today compounded over a number of years. The opportunity cost is the difference between that future value of one investment and the future value you expect to receive for the investment you actually made.

Download a complimentary calculator to further help understand this concept. Refer to the Resources section in the back of this book for more information.

Let's consider an example.

Two brothers Emilio and Farid decide to buy similar cars.

Emilio buys the red car with $20,000 from his savings. He owns the car free and clear. After ten years, Emilio sells the car for $1,000. His $20,000 saved him all the interest he would have paid for the car.

However, Farid decided to obtain a car loan from his local credit union to buy the car. His car loan along with interest payments cost him $X over the 5 year loan. He invests his $20,000 into an investment that pays him 12% for the next ten years. Farid ends up with almost $62,117 pre-tax in the ten years.

The opportunity cost is the difference between the two scenarios.

Let's use another example from earlier and give it some numbers.

Two sisters Amanda and Christine decide to each buy a $250,000 rental property. They both have $50,000 in savings.

Christine invests her $50,000 into the down payment for her rental property. She has no more savings. Assuming an appreciation rate of 6% over 30 years, her rental property will be worth approximately $1,435,873. Her mortgage should be paid off by then.

Amanda keeps her $50,000 liquid and finds an equity partner to invest the down payment for the rental property in exchange for 50% ownership. Assuming an appreciation rate of 6% over 30 years, her rental property will be worth approximately $1,435,873. Her mortgage should be paid off by then. But she has to pay her equity partner half of that, which leaves her with $717,936 and her original $50,000.

It appears that Christine had a better deal. However, that's for one property. Amanda was able to do that four times all together.

Amanda really ends up with $2,871,746 in addition to her $50,000. Furthermore, with the $50,000 in a liquid account, Amanda has piece of mind in case of emergencies and her financials still look good. Christine doesn't have that piece of mind and her financials don't look as good due to the lack of liquidity.

Let's review where we are so far.

We previously mentioned you typically have 2 options to finance things. You can either pay cash giving up the interest you would have received on your cash, or borrow money to make your purchase and pay interest to someone else.

Then we added another consideration.

How much more valuable is having cash than spending it? Another way of thinking about it is how much additional borrowed money can we access for having the cash?

Now we have to ask how we should structure a deal using raised money.

When we decide to use other people's money, we have to know how to structure the deal.

In my previous book, *The Wealthy Code*, I discuss how to structure financing for various deals. It is important you match the financing to the type of asset and the risk profile.

As an investor, you must set your guidelines to make sure money is used as efficiently as possible, especially other people's money. That depends on your underlying investments.

Here is a sample guideline:
- Considering you have Cash:
    - $50,000 or less, use it to build liquid reserve.
    - Between $50,000 and $300,000, use $200,000 for short term deals, especially for private lending and buying under market assets.
    - $300,000+ use anything above the $300,000 for longer term investments.
    - These numbers should be based on your investment. The larger your investment, the higher these numbers

across the board should be. The numbers above are for someone starting out.

- HELOC:
  - Use for short term deals (one year or less), including private lending deals among other things.
  - Do not use for a down payment except for temporary use and only until you find an equity partner and within 12 months.
- Private Money:
  - Structure as equity partners for down payments on leveraged real estate.
  - Use for short term deals as well including private lending.
  - Use for safer principal-protected investments
- Mortgage:
  - Use for acquiring properties by using 80% or less loan-to-value, fixed interest, for as long as possible (preferably 30 year), with the lowest loan constant possible. Use BER and DCR metrics to figure out the right LTV.

These are meant as <u>sample</u> guidelines.

They allow for efficient use of your capital, which in turn should translate well into six figures or more over your lifetime, and for many investors, seven figures or more.

The Family Bank

In chapter twelve, we will discuss a concept called "The Family Bank," which allows you to have yet another option. For completeness sake, I will briefly mention how the family bank is related to opportunity cost.

We started this chapter saying you have 2 main choices for any transaction. Buy it with your cash and give up the interest or borrow the money and pay interest to someone. Well, the family bank gives you a 3rd option. With this 3rd option, you can borrow money from your OWN "bank" and buy a product and then simply pay your OWN "bank" back plus interest. You end up gaining the interest while keeping your cash for investing. Very powerful.

That is further discussed in chapter twelve.

Example

Recently, someone gave me a scenario and asked for my opinion. I thought it was so interesting, I decided to share it in this book.

Four friends, Tom, James, Steve and Greg all work in the same company making the same income. They all decide to invest. However, their investment style is very different. They each decide to allocate $200 per month to invest, and they pick a horizon of 12 years to compare their investments.

FIGURE 7: FOUR FRIENDS DECIDE TO INVEST

Tom decides to save the $200 at the beginning of every month in a savings account paying 1% annually, compounded monthly. He decides that once he accumulates at least $20,000, he will buy a $20,000 asset with all the saved cash and use no debt to buy this asset. The asset appreciates 5% per year. He decides to also keep saving $200 per month into the savings account after he buys the asset.

FIGURE 8: TOM'S INVESTMENT

James decides to buy this same $20,000 asset that appreciates 5% per year with borrowed money today, and decides to use the $200 per month to pay down the loan. The loan for the asset is a 30-year amortized loan at 4% annual interest rate, compounded monthly. He also decides to keep saving $200 per month (beginning) into the savings account after he pays off the loan.

James

FIGURE 9: JAMES' INVESTMENT

Steve on the other hand decides to use a similar strategy as James but buys a $20,000 asset today with the same loan as James, but the asset doesn't appreciate at all. He too decides to also keep saving $200 at the beginning of each month into the savings account after he pays of the loan.

Steve

FIGURE 10: STEVE'S INVESTMENT

Greg decides to do exactly what James does, but instead decides to buy 2 assets of $20,000 each today using borrowed money, using similar loan terms as James. He applies the $200 per month towards both loans, $100 per month towards each loan equally.

Greg

FIGURE 11: GREG'S INVESTMENT

Who would have increased their net worth the most in 12 years?

Let's look at each of them carefully. I will include the calculations for those of you who are interested in them.

Tom's Investment:

Tom decided to save the $200 at the beginning of every month in a savings account paying 1% annually, compounded monthly. He wants to accumulate $20,000 to use to buy the asset.

It takes Tom eight years and one month to accumulate at least $20,000. He actually has an additional $213.72 more which he can keep in the savings account. He decides to buy the $20,000 asset all cash and no debt. It appreciates 5% per year for the remainder of the time (three years and 11 months).

So Tom's asset appreciates to $24,213.70 at the end of the 12-year horizon he and his buddies were talking about. However, he keeps accumulating that $200 per month for 47 more periods into the savings account. Tom has an additional $9,812.67 in his savings account.

So the end result for Tom after 12 years is this:

NAME	ASSET EQUITY	CASH	TOTAL ASSETS
Tom	$24,213.70	$9,812.67	$34,026.37
James	?	?	?
Steve	?	?	?
Greg	?	?	?

TABLE 8: RESULTS OF TOM'S INVESTMENT DECISIONS

James Investment:

James decided to buy this same $20,000 asset that appreciates 5% per year with borrowed money today, and decides to use the $200 per month to pay down the loan. The loan is a 30 year amortized loan at 4% interest rate.

James' investment appreciates to $35,917.13 in 12 years.

With James applying the $200 per month towards the loan, he would have paid off his loan in ten years and two months. He will still have 22 payments of $200 he can save into his savings account in that period. So the final result for James is that he now has an investment of $35,917.13 with $4,442.41 in cash in the savings account after 12 years.

NAME	ASSET EQUITY	CASH	TOTAL ASSETS
Tom	$24,213.70	$9,812.67	$34,026.37
James	$35,917.13	$4,442.41	$40,359.54
Steve	?	?	?
Greg	?	?	?

TABLE 9: RESULTS OF TOM'S INVESTMENT DECISIONS

James is way ahead of Tom when they both started with $200 per month!

Steve's Investment:

Steve on the other hand decided to use a similar strategy as James but buys a $20,000 asset today with the same loan as James, but the asset doesn't appreciate. So there is no need to calculate appreciation and the investment will still be $20,000 after 12 years.

Similarly, from the above calculation for James' loan, we know the loan pays off in ten years and two months. So Steve's loan is paid off in ten years and two months. He has 22 payments of $200 he can save into the savings account, giving him $4,442.41 saved up in that period.

So the final result for Steve is that he now has an investment of $20,000.00 with $4,442.41 in cash after 12 years.

NAME	ASSET EQUITY	CASH	TOTAL ASSETS
Tom	$24,213.70	$9,812.67	$34,026.37
James	$35,917.13	$4,442.41	$40,359.54
Steve	$20,000.00	$4,442.41	$24,442.41
Greg	?	?	?

TABLE 10: RESULTS OF STEVE'S INVESTMENT DECISIONS

Notice that Steve started investing early on, but invested in the wrong asset. He is trailing everyone else even though he started with the right intent.

Greg's Investment:

Greg decided to do exactly what James did, but instead decides to buy 2 assets of $20,000 each today using borrowed money, using similar loan terms as James. He applies the $200 per month towards both loans, $100 per month towards each loan equally.

We know from James' calculation that the investment appreciates to $35,917.13 after 12 years. Since Greg has two of them, both assets are now valued at $71,834.26.

Greg's payment on each loan was $95.48 per month, but he made a $100 payment to each loan. So the $100 allocated to pay each loan should suffice. Now let's see how much the loan balance for each loan would be after 12 years. The loan balance of each loan is $13,852.15 at the end of 12 years, or $27,704.24 in total for both loans. No cash in the savings account.

NAME	ASSET EQUITY	CASH	TOTAL ASSETS
Tom	$24,213.70	$9,812.67	$34,026.37
James	$35,917.13	$4,442.41	$40,359.54
Steve	$20,000.00	$4,442.41	$24,442.41
Greg	$44,130.02	$0	$44,130.02

TABLE 11: RESULTS OF GREG'S INVESTMENT DECISIONS

Overall Result:

The table below shows the final result in 12 years. Greg has the highest net worth (all else being equal), followed by James, then Tom, then Steve.

NAME	ASSET EQUITY	CASH	TOTAL ASSETS
Tom	$24,213.70	$9,812.67	$34,026.37
James	$35,917.13	$4,442.41	$40,359.54
Steve	$20,000.00	$4,442.41	$24,442.41
Greg	$44,130.02	$0	$44,130.02

TABLE 12: OVERALL RESULTS OF INVESTMENT DECISIONS

None of them started with a large savings account of money to spend. They were each comfortable with $200 per month to start. Not much. Now if we extend this to over 20 years, some of them will end up not having to work again, while others have to remain working. The difference boiled down to one single decision.

One of them saved the $200 until he had enough to purchase.

One of them purchased an asset and used the $200 to pay down the loan.

One of them purchased the wrong asset.

Finally, one of them purchased the right assets as well as the right amount of assets, and used the same as his friends $200 per month to make the payments on the loans. The decision each one made on how to use their $200 per month had huge implications and produced significantly different results.

Incidentally, none of them made the best decision, but Greg came close. Hopefully you see, as this example illustrates the importance of using your money efficiently.

When we cover inflation, you will see a whole new perspective to this exercise.

* * *

I leaned back in my chair in astonishment.

"Most people are trying to save money by cutting their expenses. Others try to make more money by working more hours or several jobs. What you just showed me is that the efficient use of your money and other people's money can beat both of those in a big way!" *I said looking at all three people at the table. They could see I was excited.*

They nodded in agreement.

"Everyone should know this!" *I gasped.*

"It's all out there, but no one wants to take the time to learn it" *said my mentor.*

He then pointed to the waiter as an example of an everyday person who could increase their net worth significantly just by simply understanding and putting this available information to use.

Your ability to increase your net worth boils down to you recognizing your lack of knowledge, you having the desire to learn what is readily available, and your willingness to unlearn all those "truths" you were taught.

Chapter Summary

- Opportunity cost is the biggest cost for most people.
- Debt allows you to move to the "Receiving" side of opportunity cost.
- The use of the <u>correct</u> debt can help you tap into more opportunities, which can result in significant wealth for you and your family.
- It is important for you to understand and be able to measure opportunity cost.
- When you purchase something, you typically have 2 main options, buy with cash and give up the interest you would have earned on that money, or borrow money to make your purchase, which means you pay a 3rd party interest. However, you can give yourself a 3rd choice by building your own family bank and using it to finance the purchase, and then you pay the purchase interest to your own family bank instead of a 3rd party financial institution.
- It is important to have guidelines for when to use what type and source of capital. An example was given in this chapter. Being able to match the right capital source to the right investment and scenario is critical. I believe everyone should have a diagram that summarizes their capital usage guidelines. It will prove very effective.

Chapter Seven

Moving to the Receiving Side of Inflation

"George, I want to go back to something we discussed earlier" Emile said. "Earlier, we discussed that if you deposit a certain amount of money monthly into your savings account, your calculator shows us we will end up with a gazillion dollars in a gazillion years! I mentioned that this is the conditioning for us to play in the financial system to benefit others. I also mentioned something called 'real' dollars."

"Remember that?" he asked. I nodded my head.

"Well that gazillion dollars will buy you LESS things in the future than today."

"In other words you will be able to buy LESS food for example in the future with that money than today" he continued.

I was so confused. How can I buy less food with my gazillion dollars?

* * *

Let's start with the basic understanding of inflation. Here's what most people know about inflation. According to the United States Department of Labor, "Inflation has been defined as a process of continuously rising prices, or equivalently, of a continuously falling value of money."

The site continues by talking about the CPI—Consumer Price Index "Various indexes have been devised to measure different aspects of inflation. The CPI measures inflation as experienced by consumers in their day-to-day living expenses. CPI is generally the best measure for adjusting payments to consumers when the intent is to allow consumers to purchase, at today's prices, a market basket of goods and services equivalent to one that they could purchase in an earlier period. It is also the best measure to use to translate retail sales and hourly or weekly earnings into real or inflation-free dollars."

So in essence, Inflation, or more precisely price inflation, is the percentage increase in the price of the "basket of goods and services" over a specific period of time. To figure out the percentage of increase, we use the CPI for our calculations. Therefore, the Consumer Price Index (CPI) is different than the inflation rate because the CPI is used to calculate the actual inflation rate.

That's the extent of what most people know.

But there are a lot more interesting things that most people don't know, and it's in these details that inflation becomes so interesting, and in fact can make you rich.

Nominal vs Real Dollars:

Let's first lay the foundation by talking about two important terms: "Nominal dollars" and "Real dollars."

Understanding these terms is critical. Before I explain them, let's start with a question to consider:

FIGURE 12: COLLECT $1,000 TODAY OR $1,500 IN 5 YEARS?

Referring to the diagram above, if you could collect $1,000 today or $1,500 in five years, which would you pick? Most people will pick randomly one of these choices. But let me give you a hint. If you had to buy something with that money, what would you buy if you collected $1,000 today or $1,500 in five years?

You probably know what you can buy with the $1,000 today, but have no idea what you can buy with the $1,500 in five years because you don't know what the pricing of various products would be in five years. The $1,000 are "real dollars" (today's dollars) and the $1,500 are "nominal dollars" (future dollars) with no idea what you could purchase with them.

Now, still without explaining the terms, let's consider another example.

FIGURE 13: COLLECT $1,000 TODAY OR $750 5 YEARS AGO?

Referring to the diagram above, if you could collect $1,000 today or could have collected $750 five years ago, which would you pick? Again, most people will pick randomly one of these choices. But let me give you a similar hint. If you had to buy something with that money, what could you buy if you collected $1,000 today or the $750 five years ago?

Again, you probably know what you can buy with the $1,000 today, but have no idea what you could have purchased with the $750 five years ago because you don't know what the pricing of various products was five years ago (or cannot recall). Again, the $1,000 is "real dollars" (today's dollars) and the $750 is in "nominal dollars" (past dollars).

Okay, let's dive in and explain those very important terms.

Think of nominal dollars as "countable" dollars. If seven years from now, you have $53,000 in your savings account, that's the "countable" amount of dollars you have - $53,000. That's how much you would count if you were to count your money. Those dollars are also known as nominal dollars. "Nominal dollars" is the amount of money (number of dollars) that you paid for something in the past, or would pay for something in the future, without accounting for inflation. Similar to how the $1,500 in the future or $750 in the past was in our previous examples. You have no idea what you could buy or could have bought with those dollars.

"Real dollars" represents how much or what that money can buy today. So if you could buy a car for $25,000 today and that identical car for $53,000 in the future, the "real dollars" of that future $53,000 is $25,000 or today's money. "Real dollars" is what you can buy using today's money—it's your "purchasing power." So "Real dollars", account for inflation, and are dollars today.

"Real dollars" means TODAY's dollars. "Nominal dollars" are FUTURE or PAST dollars without consideration for inflation.

For instance, a twelve-pack of beer may have cost $1 in 1965 "nominal dollars". Now that same twelve-pack of beer adjusted for inflation, costs $6 or $7 "real dollars." today

The way to think about it is this. If I gave you 250,000 Turkish dollars, the first question you would ask is "how much is this worth?" What you are really asking is "what can I buy with this money?" or "What is its equivalent in U.S. dollars?"

All you really care about is what you can buy with your Turkish dollars. That is why you ask the first question. You ask the second question because you know what you can buy with U.S. dollars today.

Ultimately, everything boils down to "Real dollars." "Nominal dollar" doesn't help much if you cannot translate and relate it to real dollars.

Again, think of "nominal" dollars as "countable" dollars in the past or the future, and "real" dollars as what you can buy with those past or future "nominal" dollars in today's money.

Real dollars = Purchasing power
Nominal dollars = Countable dollars

One tells you what you can purchase with it in today's money, while the other tells you how many dollars you have in the future or had in the past without consideration to what you can purchase with them.

Real dollars are more important than nominal dollars. They are also called inflation-adjusted dollars.

You can translate nominal dollars to real dollars and vice versa.

For instance, I offer to give you $100,000 in 15 years, or I offer to give you $5,000 today. Which would you pick?

Think about it.

Here's what you are thinking... "Hmmm... I can use $5,000 today to buy a laptop with a printer and an iPad, but I can have LOTS of money in 15 years!"

Well, $100,000 sounds like a lot in 15 years, but the question is in the future can it buy you MORE or LESS things than the identical laptop, printer and iPad? It seems that it could buy you more, but how do you know?

The $100,000 is "nominal" dollars and the $5,000 is "real" dollars.

You hire an expert and she tells you that with the $100,000 in the future you could buy $6,000 worth of today's stuff. The $6,000 is the equivalent "real" dollars of that nominal $100,000.

So, nominal dollars don't have a lot of significance. "Real" dollars do. Real dollars are also called inflation-adjusted dollars.

Guess what most people deal with? Yes, that's right, nominal dollars.

==The first thing to do to move over to the right side of the Wealth Equation== is for you to start ==looking at and thinking== in terms of ==real dollars.== So you have to change your thinking and become comfortable with your new way of thinking.

I have provided a spreadsheet to help you go back and forth between nominal and real dollars. Refer to the back of the book to receive the spreadsheet.

So when looking at investments and money, you need to actually think about and look at BOTH, nominal and real dollars.

Inflation makes wealth flow from the left side to the right side of the Wealth Equation thus working for you when you are positioned on the right side of the WealthQ.

Inflation makes wealth flow from the left side to the right side of the Wealth Equation.

Once you understand HOW to think about it, HOW inflation works, and HOW to make it work for you, you essentially move to the right side of the Wealth Equation and people on the left side just hand you over their wealth. I know how this sounds, but you are about to discover that on your own in this chapter.

The people on the left side of the Wealth Equation think in terms of nominal dollars, but people on the right think in terms of real dollars.

People on the left side of the Wealth Equation think in terms of nominal dollars, while people on the right think mainly in terms of real dollars.

Keep reading.

Most people think of inflation as an increase in price levels. That's not totally accurate. Inflation is actually a decrease in what our money can buy us. But since people on the left side of the WealthQ see nominal dollars, they keep counting the dollars and don't see the drop in purchasing power. The people on the right see real dollars, and understand that inflation means a drop of purchasing power.

Now that we have a basic understanding of nominal dollars and real dollars, let's take this a step further.

Thinking like the Right Side Investors

In the image below, you have $1,000 in cash, and you have a very expensive cup of coffee for $1,000. We will use that cup of coffee to represent tangible goods and services you can buy.

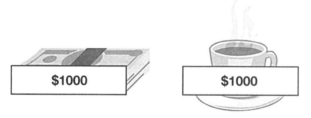

FIGURE 14: STARTING WITH $1,000 CASH. COFFEE COSTS $1,000.

Cash can be used to buy this cup of coffee.

Instead of buying the cup of coffee though, you invest that $1,000 and buy an asset for $1,000 (represented by gold bars in the image below).

FIGURE 15: STARTING WITH $1,000 CASH. COFFEE COSTS $1,000. ASSET COSTS $1,000.

Now, let's just fast forward a few years into the future, inflation doubles, and the asset now has grown to $1,700. That sounds great. However, the cup of coffee is now $2,000.

FIGURE 16: INFLATION DOUBLES. ASSET APPRECIATES TO $1,700. COFFEE COSTS $2,000.

So did you really "make" money when you cannot afford to buy the same cup of coffee? Yes, you "made" money, but you lost "purchasing power", because you cannot buy the same goods and services you could have purchased before.

You made nominal dollars (from $1,000 to $1,700), but in terms of real dollars, (purchasing power) you lost. Prior to the investment, your $1,000 cash could buy the $1000 coffee, but now, with the asset "appreciating", you cannot afford the now $2000 coffee!

It's really important to always think in terms of purchasing power and in real dollars.

So let's go back in time to the $1,000 example, and assume a friend of yours convinces you to buy another asset (bar of gold in image) because it will keep up with inflation. So you decide to buy the asset.

FIGURE 17: STARTING WITH $1,000 CASH. COFFEE COSTS $1,000. ASSET COSTS $1,000.

Now, you have a bar of gold and no cash. You could have used the money to buy the cup of coffee, but decided not to. So a few years later, inflation doubles, and the bar of gold goes up in value to $2,000. The cup of coffee is now also $2,000.

FIGURE 18: INFLATION DOUBLES. ASSET APPRECIATES TO $2,000. COFFEE COSTS $2,000.

Now the bar of gold kept up with inflation. You think you can still buy the cup of coffee now… but can you?

So you decide to sell the bar of gold and you collect your $2,000. But you purchased it for $1,000. So you have to pay taxes on your $1,000 capital gains. Assuming you are left with $700 in profit, you now have $1,700 in cash. But you cannot afford to buy the cup of coffee! It's $2,000. So you purchased an asset that "keeps up with inflation" just to find out that after taxes, you really have not kept up with inflation. You actually lost purchasing power (real dollars), and yet you still have to pay taxes on "profit" (in nominal dollars)!

The point here is that you pay taxes on nominal dollars, but there is no regard to "real dollars." Why is this important? Again, because most people on the left side think in nominal dollars.

Still, the "secret" of how the people on the right side of the Wealth Equation think is yet to be revealed. Keep reading.

The people on the left side of the Wealth Equation are thinking about what asset to buy to keep up with inflation. Even with a great asset that keeps up or beats inflation, they will still have to pay taxes on the "profit", which in turn reduces their purchasing power. In terms of "real dollars", they are losing.

Let's look at another example.

Let's say you do have $1,000, and you could have purchased the cup of coffee for the $1,000, but decided not to. You decide to hold on to your cash.

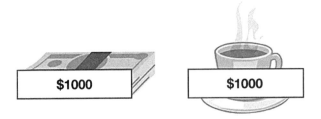

FIGURE 19: STARTING WITH $1,000. COFFEE COSTS $1,000.

A few years later that cup of coffee costs $2,000 due to inflation doubling. You are still holding on to your $1,000 cash. By doing so, now you can purchase half of what you could previously. Your purchasing power dropped in half. Your $1,000 nominal dollars is now worth $500 in real dollars. You lost half your real dollars. See image below.

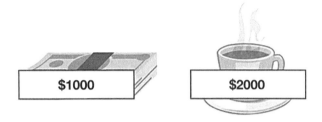

FIGURE 20: INFLATION DOUBLES. COFFEE COSTS $2,000. YOU STILL HAVE $1,000 CASH.

Notice that holding on to the cash dropped your purchasing power. This will come into play a little later. Don't forget this.

So, let's make this a little more interesting. You decide to buy an asset that beats inflation. You hire the smartest people in the world and they introduce you to an asset that beats inflation. You start doing cartwheels and decide, you will become rich with this. So, again, with the $1,000, you decide not to buy the very expensive coffee (represents goods and services), but to buy this fantastic asset that beats inflation (represented with gold bars in the image below).

FIGURE 21: STARTING WITH $1,000 CASH. COFFEE COSTS $1,000. ASSET COSTS $1,000.

A few years later, as inflation doubles, here's what you have:

FIGURE 22: INFLATION DOUBLES. ASSET APPRECIATES TO $2,200. COFFEE COSTS $2,000.

Your asset is $2,200 and the cup of coffee is $2,000. Your asset indeed beat inflation. You look in the mirror and say to yourself "I'm so smart. I'm so good looking. I have this investing thing!" You sell your asset for $2,200 and now you have to pay taxes on the gain of $1,200. Assume this is 30%, you now pay $360 in taxes. You have $1,840 left altogether. Coffee is $2,000! You cannot afford it! Hmmm. What happened? You are thinking like the investors on the left side of the WealthQ. After taxes, you still lost purchasing power even when the asset beat inflation by a good margin.

At this point, you are wondering why this is not "working"—am I doing anything weird? No. I am simply shedding some light on how investors on the right side of the WealthQ "see" things. You have been stuck on the left side of the WealthQ for too long.

Let's continue.

So you decide to try something different.

You decide to use your $1,000 to buy an asset that keeps up with inflation, but you decide to buy more of it using debt. You borrow $1,000 and use your existing $1,000 to buy $2,000 worth of this asset. Coffee at the time is $1,000.

FIGURE 23: STARTING WITH $1,000 CASH. COFFEE COSTS $1,000. YOU DECIDE TO BORROW ANOTHER $1,000 TO BUY $2,000 OF ASSETS.

So a few years later, inflation doubles. Coffee is double ($2,000) and your $2,000 asset is $4,000. Here's what things look like:

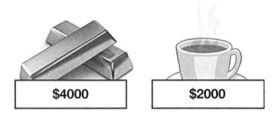

FIGURE 24: INFLATION DOUBLES. ASSET APPRECIATES TO $4,000. COFFEE COSTS $2,000.

You sell your asset of $4,000. You pay $600 in taxes on your $2,000 gain, and then pay off your $1,000 loan. You are now left with $2,400 in cash. Coffee is $2,000. You can finally afford to buy it and still keep some cash in your pocket!

This might seem like it's dragging on, but it's so important you understand this, because I'm trying to make you think differently.

What happened?

Two things changed. You used a loan and you purchased more of the assets. Which one was the differentiator? Was it the loan or the fact that we purchased more assets? Let's try the latter without the loan and see what happens.

Let's assume the following scenario. You start with $2,000 cash. You can buy $2,000 worth of assets that keep up with inflation or 2 cups of $1,000 coffee (must be good coffee!).

FIGURE 25: STARTING WITH $2,000 CASH. COFFEE COSTS $1,000. ASSET COSTS $2,000.

After a few years, inflation doubles. Coffee is $2,000 and your asset is $4,000.

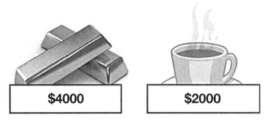

FIGURE 26: INFLATION DOUBLES. ASSET APPRECIATES TO $4,000. COFFEE COSTS $2,000.

You sell your asset and pay $600 in taxes on your $2,000 gain. You are left with $3,400. Coffee is $2,000. Previously, you were able to buy 2 cups of coffee. Now you are not able to buy 2 cups. Your purchasing power dropped even though you had purchased more assets!

So going back to the previous scenario, the only reason your purchasing power went up was because of the debt! Yes, it was the debt that increased your purchasing power. Let's keep going to understand why.

Let's analyze carefully what happened. NOW this is where things get interesting.

Remember when we discussed the holding on to the cash and the coffee doubled due to inflation? I asked you to remember it. We observed that the purchasing power in real dollars dropped to half. Remember that a few pages ago? Well, here is why I demonstrated that. The lender is lending you the money to purchase the asset, their loan amount doesn't go up (they are paid interest). This is similar to holding on to the cash in that example. A lender's loan serves as cash for us. We receive the benefit of the loan and it allows us to receive the benefit of the lender's money dropping in purchasing power. WOW!

Your initial net worth was $1,000. You purchased the asset for $2,000 by borrowing the remaining $1,000 and using your $1,000 cash.

Both the asset and the cup of coffee doubled, which means they are the same in "real dollars"—they haven't changed. Your $1,000 didn't really increase your purchasing power, it maintained it.

But your $1,000 loan that was used to buy the asset is now worth half the real dollars from when you purchased the asset (relative to the coffee). Refer back to the cash example mentioned earlier. Inflation doubled, but the loan amount stayed the same.

So your profit in nominal dollars is $1,000 (you sold the asset for $2,000, and paid off the $1,000 loan). However, the $1,000 represents $500 worth of purchasing power (it can only buy half the cup of coffee).

So by buying the asset with a loan of $1,000, you increased your net worth in real dollars by $500. When you purchased the asset with all cash, you ended with the same purchasing power— no increase in net worth in real dollars!

Let's consider one more scenario. The same as above, but with a loan we purchase an asset that doesn't keep up with inflation.

You start again with $1,000 cash. Coffee is $1,000. The asset is $1,000. You decide to purchase the asset (that doesn't keep up with inflation but does indeed appreciate). You borrow $1,000 to buy it along with your $1,000 cash. You buy a $2,000 asset.

FIGURE 27: STARTING WITH $1,000 CASH. COFFEE COSTS $1,000. YOU DECIDE TO BORROW $1,000 ALONG WITH YOUR $1,000 CASH TO BUY $2,000 OF ASSETS.

After a few years, inflation doubles. Coffee is now $2,000. The $2,000 asset is now $3,900, but would have been $4,000 if it had kept up with inflation. But it didn't keep up with inflation.

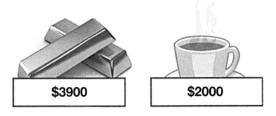

FIGURE 28: INFLATION DOUBLES. ASSET APPRECIATES TO $3900. COFFEE COSTS $2,000.

At first glance, it looks like the investment didn't perform well overall. You sell the asset for $3,900. Your capital gain is $1,900. You pay $590 in taxes leaving $1,330 in after taxes profit. You pay off your loan and receive your initial $1,000 investment back, leaving you with $2,330 in cash. Coffee though is $2,000! You increased your purchasing power even though the asset didn't keep up with inflation!

Again, it's the debt that makes you rich, not the asset!

So what is the "aha" here?

The PROFIT is not in the asset appreciation, it is in the LOAN. The LOAN is where the profit is. Debt is what makes you rich!

The asset just keeps up with inflation; the loan is the secret sauce to profiting from inflation!

So let's go back to the Wealth Equation. The "investors" on the left side are looking for the assets to purchase, but the people on the right side are looking for the right financing for their assets. They know how to match the assets to the right loans. The key is picking the right LOAN, a well-structured loan. The investors on the right side understand that having the right loan is better any day over just having the right asset like those looked for by the people on the left.

Let's take an example.

We have two friends Sandra and Kate. They each have $50,000 saved up and decide to invest.

Sandra uses her $50,000 to buy an asset she believes will beat inflation.

Kate uses her $50,000 to buy a $100,000 asset that doesn't even keep up with inflation, and ends up borrowing $50,000 to buy it. She understands that the secret to wealth is in the loan, not the asset.

A few years later, inflation doubles. A $1,000 cup of coffee is now $2,000. So the $50,000 asset Sandra purchased is now $100,000. The one that Kate purchased is now $200,000. Let's look at the results.

Sandra's investment actually does beat inflation, and the asset is now worth $105,000. She beat inflation by $5,000. What used to be $50,000 is now $100,000, but she has a $105,000 asset! She sells it, and has a nominal profit of $55,000. Remember, she pays taxes of nominal dollars, not real dollars. Assuming she pays $16,500 in taxes, she is left with $88,500 altogether. She lost in real dollars, but profited in nominal dollars. With that money, she cannot buy the goods and services she was able to buy when she had the $50,000 even though her asset beat inflation!

Kate on the other hand has a very different result. Her asset did not keep up with inflation. Her $100,000 asset only appreciated to

$175,000 even though inflation doubled. With that, she cannot buy the same goods and services that also doubled. But let's keep going.

She sells the asset, and has a profit of $75,000 of nominal dollars even though she lost in terms of real dollars. She has to pay taxes on her nominal dollars profit. She pays $22,500 in taxes. She is left with $152,500, from which she has to pay off the $50,000 loan. Now she has $102,500. She started with $50,000. What used to cost $50,000 is now $100,000. So she actually beat inflation by $2,500 in nominal dollars even after taxes and even though the asset didn't keep up with inflation!

Why? Because of the loan!

So let's summarize the deal with Sandra and Kate.

Sandra purchased an asset that beat inflation and she wound up losing real dollars (purchasing power).

Kate purchased an asset that didn't keep up with inflation, yet she wound up making a profit in real dollars!

Again, Kate understands how to think like the people on the right side of the Wealth Equation!

What people on the left side don't realize is that the people on the right side are SHIFTING profits to themselves by knowing HOW to use the system then making it work for them.

Let's take this to another level.

Many people on the left side continue to "invest" in various assets such as stocks, bonds, mutual funds, and real estate among other things by focusing on the asset to earn for them a "good return." They take huge risks in their investments for a good return.

The people on the right side of the Wealth Equation know that they can take a lot less risk by using the right tools (debt) to increase their net worth without taking high risk like the people on the left.

Regarding inflation and depending on which side of the WealthQ they are; people see things from an entirely different perspective.

LEFT SIDE OF WEALTHQ	RIGHT SIDE OF WEALTHQ
Focus on asset	Focus on financing
Higher risk to earn a better return	Better financing with lower risk asset for a better return
Pays higher taxes due to focus on nominal dollars	Pays lower taxes due to focus on real dollars
Whole system works against them	Whole system works for them

TABLE 13: COMPARING LEFT SIDE AND RIGHT SIDE OF WEALTHQ IN REGARDS TO INFLATION

Let's keep digging.

Turning Inflation to Work For You

So it's clear from the previous pages that loans help you build your net worth and buffer you from inflation. Now, let's try to understand a little bit more about HOW that happens.

Debt allows you to buy an asset today, but pay for it in the future. The reason this is important is that this is where nominal dollars and real dollars come into play. When you buy an asset today using well-structured debt, you are buying it with real dollars today, but paying for it in nominal dollars in the future!

Read that again. Slowly.

> **When you buy an asset today using well-structured debt, you are buying it with real dollars today, but paying for it in nominal dollars in the future!**

Let's expand on that.

Say you buy a $100,000 asset today with a $20,000 down payment and $80,000 debt. Your debt terms are 5% interest amortized over 30 years, with monthly payments of $429.46.

Assume today the $429.46 can buy you an iPad. In 30 years, $429.46 will probably buy you the iPad case that you buy for $50 today. So you are paying $429.46 monthly for 30 years (nominal dollars). However, you own the asset in terms of real dollars today.

Over time, the asset maintains its "real value" (meaning rising with time) but you are still paying in nominal dollars. That gives you a spread that allows you to automatically increase your net worth. So in essence, you are paying back with devalued dollars.

Not Just Any Debt

Now knowing debt is good for you against inflation, the key then is what is the best type of debt to fight inflation?

Simple. Fixed interest-rate loans with as long a period as possible, which translates to the lowest annual loan constant.

> **Well-structured debt for inflation should have a fixed interest rate, be for as long a time period as possible, with the lowest loan constant you can negotiate.**

For example:
- Buy a property with a 30-year fixed-interest amortized loan over a 15-year fixed-interest amortized loan.
- Pick fixed-interest loan over an adjustable-interest loan.
- If you have to pay $5,000 in loan fees in today's dollars (real dollars) versus $5,000 in future dollars (nominal dollars), pick the latter.

Who Are The Losers From Inflation?

In an economy where inflation is rising quickly, there are many losers. Everyone on the left side of the WealthQ is losing.

Here is a list of people losing the most:

<u>Savers</u>: People savings money in checking accounts, savings accounts, certificates of deposits, etc. The interest rates do not keep up with inflation.

<u>Retirees</u>: Many retirees have their fixed income payments coming in from their "nest egg" and their "safer" portfolio. Inflation erodes the value of both their "nest egg" savings and their "safer" portfolio.

<u>Credit card debt holders</u>: Most credit cards have a variable interest rate tied to a major index such as the prime rate. This affects them negatively. Credit card holders end up experiencing quickly climbing rates and higher payments.

<u>Consumers</u>: Consumers on a set salary will feel the crunch right away from dramatically higher inflation.

<u>Investors</u>: Investors in long-term bonds. In a high-inflation environment, bonds work against you.

* * *

I was not sure how to absorb this information.

The first shock was that the people on the left side of the WealthQ "count" money differently from the people on the right side. The people on the "Paying" side "count" in "nominal" dollars, while the affluent on the right side "count" in "real" dollars. That was so different and also so important to know.

The second shock was that people on the "Paying" side purchased assets to make them rich, but those assets when looked at in "real" dollars and after taxes, are at best at break even or losing purchasing power. It's actually in the DEBT that profit is made, not the asset.

The third shock to me was that an asset doesn't even have to keep up with inflation to "make" money if it has the right debt, structured correctly.

Finally, one statement that Emile made originally threw me off, but was now starting to make sense. "The people on the "Paying" side of the WealthQ borrow money to buy assets, or buy these assets with all cash and no debt, but the people on the "Receiving" side of the WealthQ create the right debt by finding the right assets to encumber them." It was a complete switch. The left side buys assets thinking it is the assets that make them rich. The right side creates debt with the right assets because they know it is the debt that makes them wealthy.

WOW!

I had finally started to see that it was debt, indeed correctly structured debt that was the key to wealth. I finally felt everything was starting to make sense.

But there was more to come… lots more!

Chapter Summary

- It's really important to understand "nominal" dollars versus "real" dollars before trying to understand inflation.
- Real dollars means in TODAY's dollars. Nominal dollars means FUTURE or PAST dollars without consideration to inflation.
- Think of "Real dollars" as "Purchasing power" and "Nominal dollars" as "Countable dollars." One tells you what you can purchase in today's money, while the other tells you how many dollars you have in the future or in the past without consideration to what you can purchase with it.
- Real dollars are also called inflation-adjusted dollars.
- Inflation makes wealth flow from the left side to the right side of the Wealth Equation.
- People on the left side of the Wealth Equation think in terms of nominal dollars, but people on the right think in real dollars mainly.
- Well-structured debt is the key to moving to the right side of the Wealth Equation.
- When you buy an asset today using well-structured debt, you are buying it in real dollars today, but paying for it in nominal dollars in the future!
- Well-structured debt for inflation should be at a fixed interest rate for as long a period as possible. Aim for the lowest loan constant you can get.

Chapter Eight

Lowering Your Taxes

"So let's talk about the exciting world of taxes" Emile said sarcastically as he smiled.

My body reacted negatively. I disliked dealing with taxes, but I knew I had to "deal with it." So I reluctantly leaned over. "You don't seem to like the topic of taxes" he chuckled. I shared with him my dislike of dealing with taxes and the overly-complicated nature of it.

"Well then, I will share with you my simple system to dealing with taxes" he said.

I was expecting Emile to go over a whole bunch of deductions and numbers.

He proceeded to share with me his system for dealing with taxes that was pretty powerful. I always enjoyed "systems", and this system was one that I could use for taxes.

He called it his "Tax Management System".

* * *

In chapter three, we saw how devastating taxes can be on your portfolio.

When we looked at our doubling of a penny problem, we noticed that the results were pretty outstanding.

Here were the results:

- Tax-Free Compounding Growth: penny turns into $5,368,709.12.
- Tax-Deferred Compounding Growth: penny turns into $3,758,096.38 (assuming 30% bracket).
- Taxable Compounding Growth: penny turns into $48,196.86 (assuming 30% bracket).

Obviously, we cannot find a place to double our penny every day, but this illustrates the magnitude taxes can have on our investments.

The affluent on the right side of the Wealth Equation know that and therefore plan for it.

There are tax benefits offered by the government to business owners, and it's important that you find the right experts to help you maximize your tax benefits. Many people try to figure out their own tax savings in order to save money. I cannot stress the importance of having the right professionals on your team to help do that instead of you doing it yourself.

Also, beyond tax savings is what you do with your savings. Most people spend them, while people on the right side of the WealthQ reinvest them.

A tax savings of $5,000 in one year will result in over $50,000 in 30 years compounded at 8%, and that's just a one-time tax savings. Each $5,000 used correctly as described in this book can result in even a higher amount in the same time frame.

Again, the key is to have the right team work on your taxes. Unfortunately, most people think that just means having an accountant. Most accountants look through your existing taxes to find tax deductions. However, the right tax attorney or tax professional (which I will refer to as "tax strategist" later) for example can restructure things and create new entities to create new tax deductions and therefore generate bigger tax benefits. So don't just go to your accountant and assume you are done, rather, find the right tax professional, typically a tax attorney. The cost might be higher for the latter, but they more than pay for themselves with their tax planning and savings knowledge.

The key is to have as much of your investment growing in a tax-deferred or tax-free environment.

Furthermore the use of debt strategically has tax benefits. This includes mortgages, business debt, HELOCs used for certain things, and loans for investments. Not all loan interest qualifies as a tax deduction, but it is always prudent to see if a new loan will qualify as one. Consult with your tax professional as to deductibility of interest before using debt for an investment.

The strategic use of debt may have tax benefits. Work with your tax professional.

I could show you lots of charts on how tax-deferred and tax-free environments can save you a lot of money, but I will not do that. Also, I will not talk about how you should not do your own taxes or actual benefits, but rather I will share with you the basics of the system the affluent have in place to address taxes. The system is called the "Tax Management System."

So let's jump in.

The Four Components of the Tax Management System

FIGURE 29: THE FOUR COMPONENTS OF THE TAX MANAGEMENT SYSTEM

Here are the four components for your Tax Management System:

Team: This is your TEAM that should be involved in all aspects of your Tax Management System and responsible for helping increase your net-worth and save you money. The team should work together for and with you. The team should work off of your "Big Picture" plan for your taxes! You need to lead this team by following a plan that one of your team members (the Tax Strategist) develops for you in writing. We will discuss who should be on your team later in this chapter.

Plan: The PLAN is customized for you by your Tax Strategist. It should include the entities to use and instructions on how to use them. It should also be straight forward and clearly written so that anyone in the future can follow it. It should have measurable, defined benefits (savings), and it should be written to be useful for many years to come.

Vehicles: Your VEHICLES can/should include whatever your Tax Strategist thinks would be best for you, such as trusts, qualified retirement plans, banking systems, entities etc.

Processes: Your PROCESSES are all the processes that you will need to have in place for running a very efficient system. These include systems for filing, tracking expenses, documentation, verification, bookkeeping process etc.

The Three Team Members of Your Tax Management System

FIGURE 30: THE THREE MAIN TEAM MEMBERS IN THE TAX MANAGEMENT SYSTEM

Here are the 3 team members of your Tax Management System:

- **Tax Strategist**
- **Accountant**
- **Bookkeeper**

This is the team that would be involved in all aspects of your Tax Management System and responsible for helping increase your net-worth and save you money. All team members should work together for you. All three should review and work off of your "Big Picture" plan for your taxes! You need to lead this team by instructing your Tax Strategist to first develop your "Big Picture" plan for you in writing, then getting your accountant on board and have them discuss your plan, and finally your bookkeeper. A payroll service is sometimes added to this to handle just that, your payroll.

Here's a brief description of each of these functions:

> **Tax Strategist:** There is not a specific "Tax Strategist" designation. A Tax Strategist is a CPA or Tax Attorney who has studied how to predict the tax consequences of business and investment decisions. The primary difference between a good CPA and a Tax Strategist is time. A CPA/Tax Strategist can lay out a course of tax loopholes that steer you clear of tax situations, legally. A good tax CPA catches you after you've run into the problems and then helps you get

out of them. A Tax Strategist helps build your "Big Picture" plan (sometimes called your "Tax Strategy Plan") that your Accountant and Bookkeeper can use to save you taxes. You should meet with them at least once a year, and more often as they recommend which will depend on your business.

Accountant: Accountants' work varies depending on if they work in a company as an employee or on their own where they may focus on assisting small businesses.

Some accountants are directly involved in preparing an organization's financial statements. Other accountants work with a corporation's management in analyzing costs of operations, and products. This can also involve budgeting and preparing reports. Some accountants and CPAs choose to work on their own and focus on assisting small businesses with their accounting systems, financial statements, income tax returns, tax planning, etc. The important thing here is to make sure that your accountant works within the scope of the plan developed by your Tax Strategist.

Bookkeeper: Performs work, including but not limited to performing work of a diverse nature; serving as a bookkeeper; purchasing materials and equipment; conducting invoice activities; paying vendors for delivered materials; providing inventory support; and performing clerical/administrative functions. Bookkeepers work closely with accountants.

The Fives Phases for Launching Your Tax Management System

FIGURE 31: THE FIVE PHASES OF LAUNCHING YOUR TAX MANAGEMENT SYSTEM

Here are the phases of your tax management system:

1. **Team Building:** This is the first critical part of building your team. Your first team member should be your Tax Strategist and/or Accountant. They will help you with identifying and recruiting the other team members.

2. **Evaluation:** Meet with your Tax Strategist and go through your current financials showing where you are at this point. The reviews performed during the evaluation phase are critical for laying the groundwork to be able to move to the next phase—planning.

3. **Planning:** After the evaluation phase, the Tax Strategist can now help build a plan with a customized strategy just for you to save you on taxes and help position your financials in the best light for borrowing from the bank for investing.

4. **Strategy:** The result of the planning session is a customized strategy just for you to save you on taxes and help position your financials. This should be shared with your whole Tax Management System team, i.e. the bookkeeper, accountant and your attorney.

5. **Management:** This is your ongoing processes to follow through with your plan. This includes regular updates with your team, as well as processes in your business to keep track of documentation and verification, etc.

The team should be able to help you build your processes and checklists. Work closely with your bookkeeper to help setup your processes and checklists.

As I said this was intended as an overview of the "Tax Management System." It is important to remember that you have to focus on developing the system to solve the specific problem, in this case lowering your taxes. The cost of this system should pay for itself with the tax savings if you build the right team.

Built in Tax Savings when on the Right Side of the WealthQ

In the previous chapter on inflation, there was a very interesting implied strategy that is built into the discussed strategy. Investors on the left side of the WealthQ focus on increasing their net worth by looking at nominal dollars. "Buy something today and sell it in the future for a larger amount." As mentioned, that is the left side of WealthQ thinking. It is in nominal dollars. And as shown, they pay taxes on nominal dollars even though the purchasing power went down or stayed the same! Think about it: They are paying taxes on "gains" that don't exist in terms of real dollars!

Investors on the right side of the WealthQ look at real dollars, and focus on the debt and not "appreciation" only. In fact, because the asset doesn't have to appreciate as much, the amount of taxes paid on the nominal dollars is less than otherwise paid but the true gain is made in the real dollars from the debt, and they do NOT pay taxes on that! So as a result, the investors on the right side of the WealthQ end up paying less taxes overall and have bigger gains than the people on the left side!

To wrap up this chapter, do what the people on the right side of the WealthQ do:

- Build the right team
- Have a plan developed by your team
- Create a system to manage your taxes
- Reinvest your tax savings.
- Educate yourself. There are many books out there on this subject, it's a great idea to read a few.
- Use debt strategically.
- Place your investments in tax-advantaged environments.

* * *

"I love this system Emile!" I exclaimed. *"This helps investors feel empowered."*

"Emile has everything systemized. This is one of many systems" my mentor chuckled.

Weeks later, I was surprised to receive a box of Emile's documented systems. This box included his *"Tax Management System"*, *"Debt Management System"*, *"Credit Management System"*, *"Inflation Management System"*, and *"Family Bank System"* among many others.

These documents really shed light on how this man thinks.

Chapter Summary

- Taxes can have a devastating impact on our wealth
- The affluent on the right side of the Wealth Equation know that and therefore plan for it. They do so by doing the following:
    o Build the right team
    o Use a system to manage their taxes
    o Use debt strategically
    o Place their investments in tax-advantaged environments
    o Educate themselves
    o They know that it is important to reinvest their tax savings and not just spend them carelessly.

Section Three

Putting it All Together

Chapter Nine

Debt Revisited

As I sat there contemplating what I had learned, I realized the power of moving over to the "Receiving" side of the Wealth Equation. You position everything to work for you, and by everything I mean people, systems, money, monetary systems and the economy. That was just amazing.

"The WealthQ Method" of investing is indeed very different from traditional investing. It is a very methodical process and has a lot of thought behind it.

And the secret "weapon" behind The WealthQ Method is well-structured debt, the same thing many people say to avoid. For many people DEBT is a 4-letter word. It dawned on me that the middle class and poor people were saying that, yet the wealthy always said it was part of their "ammunition," in fact their "secret" weapon.

The words used to describe debt as a "weapon" and "ammunition" started making sense. Debt is used to fight a lot of things, but also, like any weapon, it can be used for good and bad. In fact it was debt that the ultra-wealthy used to shift wealth from the left side to the right side, thus the terms they used, "Paying" side and "Receiving" side.

But _not_ knowing how to use this weapon could really harm you.

And that is EXACTLY the problem with most people today, they simply were not trained to USE it. The wealthy knew how to obtain the weapon, control it, measure it, and ultimately use it to become wealthy.

So the problem isn't debt itself, but rather HOW to use debt.

He or she, whoever masters debt, wins. Pure and simple.

He or she who plays with fire without being trained will hurt themselves. The same is true with debt.

My mentor went on to fill in the gaps in my understanding of what we had covered that day. He explained that most people who mastered debt in conjunction with The WealthQ Method could reach financial freedom much faster than those without that mastery.

He explained that most people think it's the ASSET that they purchase that makes the difference. But the reality is different. The asset and the debt both fit into the bigger game of FINANCE. It's a financing game, and the game pieces (think of Lego) such as assets and debts have to fit together to fit your financial goals.

The WealthQ Method was a holistic method, taking into consideration how the finance game worked, and built to make the system work for you the investor.

The mindset for most people is to borrow money (debt) to be able to buy an asset. That's the wrong approach. The more effective way is to establish the correct type and amount of debt and equity against a stable asset to help generate a specific goal.

You don't buy a brick for the sake of owning a brick, but rather to build something. Assets are just a brick of the bigger picture. Debt is another. They have to be matched to fit well together to build a stable and strong foundation (also known as capital structure— more on that later).

In fact the debt is where wealth is created, not the asset. The asset just allows you to obtain the debt.

It boils down to this...

The wealthy use debt strategically. They obtain the debt against low risk and stable assets.

The rest of us use it as a necessary evil to buy assets, typically assets with a lot of volatility (higher risk).

I recalled a conversation with my mentor that afternoon. He used an analogy to explain debt as follows.

"If you want to drive from San Jose to New York, would you drive a slow car or a fast car?"

"Fast car, of course" I chuckled.

"What if your loved ones said to you that you should drive a slow car because it's safer, what would you say George?" he responded promptly.

"I would say then I wouldn't want to drive, or I would say I would drive the fast car, but drive it at a pace where I feel comfortable. Just because it's a fast car, I wouldn't drive fast. But I would have the choice to drive a little faster than SLOW if I wanted" I replied.

He paused. I could see the wheels spinning in his mind. He was trying to compose how to say whatever he was going to say next.

He smiled and said in a slow pace "George, what you just said is incredibly powerful. With a fast car, you have a choice but with the slow car, you don't. So pay attention to what I am about to ask you he said…"

"What controls the speed at which you drive?" he asked cautiously.

"Me, the driver?" I questioned.

"Yes, but HOW do you control the speed of the car?" he asked as he leaned forward.

"The gas pedal?" I questioned. I wasn't sure what he was getting at.

"Exactly George, you have the OPTION of controlling the speed of the car with the gas pedal. So is the fast car dangerous if you drive it at your own pace or even slow?"

"No" I said confidently.

"So what you are saying George is that the fast car is not dangerous if you control the speed with the gas pedal, but can be dangerous if you press the gas pedal all the way down and cannot control the car?"

"That's correct" I replied. I still wasn't sure where he was going with that.

"So let me ask you this George. Think about it carefully. When someone says a fast car is dangerous, are they saying the car itself is dangerous, the gas pedal itself is dangerous, or is the dangerous part the careless driver who is not properly trained on how to drive a fast car fast?" he asked as he smiled again.

"That's really interesting. I never thought of it that way, but it's really the careless driver that is dangerous, not the car, nor the gas pedal. But what does the gas pedal have to do with this, and where is this leading to?" I asked.

"George, the gas pedal is the debt. The debt affects how fast you go. If you drive too fast, that means you are using too much debt. The car is the asset. The gas pedal is debt. But it's the careless driver that's the danger. When people tell you that debt is bad, they are telling you the gas pedal is dangerous. They prefer you drive the slow car to New York. In fact, with no gas pedal, they are telling you to walk to New York! Because debt helps you move at a faster pace, and so having no debt, you have no gas pedal to press down. You are walking to New York" he explained.

It was making sense.

"Debt is not the problem. The asset is not problem. The careless operator is. Knowledge is what makes all the difference."

Debt is the gas pedal on a car.

It all made sense.

Debt was never the enemy. It was simply how fast you wanted to move towards your financial goals.

You can move slowly towards your goals, or you can master debt and move much faster towards them.

Or you can choose to call debt "risky" and be ignorant.

Knowledge was the biggest differentiation factor here. Debt was a tool, a very powerful tool. It wasn't the enemy. It was my ally if I simply took the time to study and master it.

He would eventually take this understanding to a whole new level... Mastering debt was a lot more than just "good debt" and "bad debt"—it was science and art at the same time.

My perspective was completely changed.

It would change my life.

I went from thinking about buying assets with debt to strategically using the right amount and the right structure of debt against the right asset to move me to the right side.

That was a complete mind-shift.

I also started understanding how debt was allowing me to play the "arbitrage" game between real dollars and nominal dollars. It allowed me to hugely benefit from that.

And the best part was how much less in taxes I would pay when playing with real dollars because the tax code was based on nominal dollars.

I chose to use debt as my strategic way to build wealth. It was now my secret weapon. I now knew, in fact, it is so much harder to build wealth without it—almost impossible actually.

It was time I learned to become a "Debt Millionaire."

Chapter Summary

- Debt can be used to make you rich or destroy you. Not knowing how to use debt could really harm you.
- The problem isn't debt itself, but rather HOW it is used.
- People think it's the ASSET that they purchase that makes them rich. It's not. It's much more than that. It is the asset, the debt and the way they are put together, among other things in the bigger game of FINANCE. It's ALL these components together that can make you rich.
- "Debt Millionaires" are the investors that understand how to use debt strategically to build wealth.

Chapter Ten

The Third Secret Side– The Key to Wealth

My mentor had drawn this diagram on a blank piece of paper. He referred to it as the 3-step process he uses in identifying the assets he would focus on to generate the result he was looking for, whether it was to generate income or growth in his portfolio. It was part of The WealthQ Method.

RESULT (step 1)	CASH FLOW ("Income")	CAPITAL GAINS ("Growth")
FRAMEWORK (step 2)	Characteristics to generate income ("Wealth Pairs")	Characteristics to increase net-worth ("Equity Pairs")
VEHICLES (step 3)	What vehicles meet the above characteristics?	What vehicles meet the above characteristics?

TABLE 14: ASSET IDENTIFYING SYSTEM

He called it "The Emile Approach."

"Prepare to step into the Matrix" he laughed as he started drawing a triangle to the right of the diagram above.

* * *

Most people on the left side of the WealthQ approach investing by picking some investment vehicle they like, for example "I like stocks, I'm going to invest in stocks" or "I like real estate, I'm going to invest in real estate." They start by almost randomly picking a vehicle to invest in. That's exactly what NOT to do. That's the wrong approach. They will only find out the result of that random act many years later, and time is one thing we cannot afford to waste in this life!

Referring to the table above, they start by picking "Vehicles" first (or assets), but as you can see in the table, that is step 3 in the process, not step 1. The table shows you the right order of the steps, starting from step 1 through step 3.

When trying to identify which assets to invest in, "don't fall in love with the asset, fall in love with the result"—so follow the system. Start with the result you are looking for, then build a framework that identifies the financial characteristics you need to accomplish the result you need, then find out which assets meet your criteria you built in your framework.

So let's start with step 1.

Step 1: Pick the Result First

The right way to approach this is to decide on the result you are seeking first, "Cash Flow" or "Capital Gains." Your portfolio should have both. These are also known as "Income" and "Growth." One of them generates income and the other increases in value over time. For example, typically people might consider bonds for income and stocks for growth (that's a simplistic example). Another way to think of them is "Income" is used to pay for your monthly expenses and "Growth" increases your net worth over time. Again, you need both in your portfolio. This is covered in more detailed in my previous book *The Wealthy Code*.

> **Your portfolio should have both INCOME and GROWTH assets. Each of these results will have its own framework.**

Step 2: Build the Framework to Accomplish the Result

Once you decide which side you want to strengthen (the result you are looking for) from step 1, then focus on building a framework (the characteristics) to generate that result. That's step 2. The framework you build to accomplish the goal for step 1 ("Cash Flow" or "Capital Gains") will help filter out many of the vehicles in step 3 and also help you decide which vehicles will help you accomplish your step 1 result.

Think of the framework as a filter. This filter allows you to identify which assets will help you meet the result you want. The filter is nothing more than a set of checklists and rules of thumb that you can use to identify which assets to use to accomplish your desired result.

The framework you build to accomplish the "Cash Flow" goal is called a "Wealth Pair Framework." The framework you build to accomplish the "Capital Gains" goal is called an "Equity Pair Framework." These are discussed in my previous book *The Wealthy Code*.

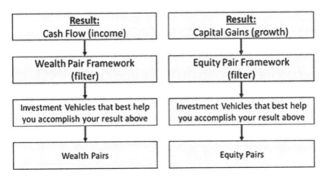

FIGURE 32: THE EMILE APPROACH

In the diagram above, the Emile Approach is shown slightly differently. Starting from the top, you identify the desired result, then you move down to create the filter to support the result you are looking for. That filter will be either a "Wealth Pair Framework" or as "Equity Pair Framework." Once determined, you run various assets through the checklist, and that exercise should help you identify which assets best fit your checklist, which in turn will support the result you are looking for. Your selections once identified, when combined with the capital to acquire them will result in the "Wealth Pairs" or "Equity Pairs" you need to generate the result you are looking for.

For "Capital Gains," you will need an "Equity Pair Framework." For "Cash Flow", you will need a "Wealth Pair Framework."

"Wealth Pairs" generate cash flow. "Equity Pairs" generate equity.

Each "pair" consists of two things; the capital and the asset.

They are "pairs" because we are combining two things, the ASSET and the CAPITAL to buy the asset (money).

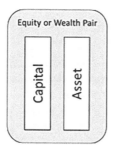

FIGURE 33: THE TWO COMPONENTS OF A WEALTH OR EQUITY PAIR

This is discussed in detail in my book *The Wealthy Code*. However, the terms "Wealth Pair" and "Equity Pair" might be a little misleading.

Why?

Because there's a hidden 3rd side and it is more like the glue that connects the two sides. They are called "pairs" because there are two physical things, the asset and the capital, but the 3rd non-physical side is as important if not more important!

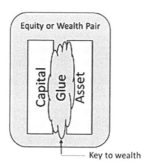

FIGURE 34: THE HIDDEN THIRD SIDE IN A WEALTH OR EQUITY PAIR

Think of it this way. Refer to the image below. You have a pile of money on one side from various sources, and an asset that you can purchase on the other side (represented by bars of gold in the image). The question is how do you structure the payments to those people investing all that money? How much profit do you give them? These are just two of the key questions you have to address. That's the "glue" that binds the pile of capital with the asset you are about to purchase.

FIGURE 35: CAPITAL & ASSET. THE MISSING "GLUE" IS THE CAPITAL STRUCTURE

This 3rd side, "the glue", is known as the "capital structure" and this is where most people fail. It's loosely called "deal structuring" but it's more specifically "capital structuring." So to expand on the previous example, this third side addresses questions such as:

- How much debt versus equity should we have on the capital side?
- How much can we afford to pay for each debt and for equity, and what are the exact terms of each.
- What are the characteristics of the asset we are looking for on the asset side?

I normally draw a triangle to represent this. Remember, here we are just focused on building step 2 to accomplish our result from step 1.

THE THIRD SECRET SIDE—THE KEY TO WEALTH

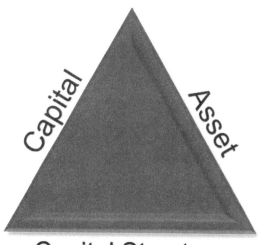

Capital Structure

FIGURE 36: THREE SIDES TO AN INVESTMENT

You will notice in the diagram the pair (capital and asset) and the capital structure that binds the two sides. This is true for every investment we ever do. For example, the asset could be real estate (rental property). The capital is what's used to buy that asset. The capital structure addresses how much debt we are borrowing, how much equity we are raising, what the terms of the loan are, etc. This is critical not just for the investment, but for moving us to the right side of the WealthQ.

Read that last sentence again! Five times if you have to. It's very eye opening!

Most people don't realize the significance of the "glue"—the capital structure. It is one of the most important aspects to building your wealth. It has to move you to the right side of the WealthQ. It has to lower your risk, and move you towards the result you selected in step 1 in the most efficient manner possible. Most investors that have attended our professional training events nationwide have never even heard of nor known of this concept!

The three sides to any investment: Capital, Asset and Capital Structure, sometimes referred to as "Deal Structure."

Capital Structure is simply how an asset is financed. In simple terms, this includes how much of the capital is debt and equity.

So let's dig a little deeper.

The framework you build in step 2 is so much more than a filter to generate the result you are seeking in step 1. It has to take into consideration everything we discussed in this book so far in terms of inflation, interest, taxes, opportunity cost, etc. This work of building the framework is done one time, and then moving forward, the framework is used to filter the assets and the capital structure to help accomplish the desired result as well as take everything in this book into consideration automatically!

For "Cash Flow", as mentioned, the characteristics ("Wealth Pair") are discussed in my previous book called *The Wealthy Code*. In that book, I shared how to use debt to generate passive income and how to create spreads by looking at metrics such as annual loan constants and capitalization rates. I also talked about other metrics to measure risk, volatility of income, etc. In fact, many investors around the country have specifically said that just knowing this information from our live trainings they have attended has significantly improved their investing.

The Capital Structure has to move you to the right side of WealthQ, it has to lower your risk, give you the best return for the risk you selected, and move you towards the result you identified in step 1, all in the most efficient manner possible.

In my previous book *The Wealthy Code*, I focused more on "Wealth Pairs" and touched on "Equity Pairs." In this book, I'm filling in some of the gaps for both of them, but more specifically the "Equity Pairs."

The main thing to realize is that the capital structure for Equity Pairs must move you to right side of the WealthQ and start increasing your net-worth automatically.

Structuring Equity Pairs:

So how do you go about building the framework for Equity Pairs? Here's a simplified framework. Let's discuss each side; the asset side and the capital side separately:

1. Asset Side: Your asset needs to have the following characteristics:

    a. You should be able to obtain a loan against it (preferably you should be able to "encumber it" with a loan). There are ways around it, but this would simplify it. In simple terms, this means you should be able to find a lender that will lend to you against this asset. You are not able to "encumber" all assets.

    b. The asset must appreciate in value over time. It would be great if it kept up with inflation, but that is NOT required, since the profit is made on the debt side, as discussed earlier.

c. The asset must have low volatility in value. You don't want something that fluctuates wildly like the stock market. You are looking for assets that are relatively stable such as real estate.

   d. The asset should be income-producing to pay for the debt, even if it's breakeven (income covers expenses and loan payments). Being income-producing is highly recommended, but not required, however it makes things so much easier if it is.

   e. The asset must allow for long term hold, ten years or more if need be.

2. Capital Side: This money needs to have the following:

   a. The money side might have to be divided into debt and equity.

   b. The debt must be long term and match with your holding period. If you want to hold the asset for 20 years, the loan must be a 20-year loan or longer.

   c. The debt must have the lowest annual loan constant possible. Refer to my book *The Wealthy Code* for an explanation. This is a requirement.

   d. The debt must be (preferably) a fixed interest rate for duration of the loan, or at least for the duration you plan on holding the asset.

   e. It is preferred (but not required) that the interest rate on the loan be lower or equal to the projected appreciation rate of the asset.

   f. The amount of debt (loan to value) should be set no higher than an amount where there is enough cushion to cover any fluctuation in the income. There are several metrics for this. For advanced investors, mainly, the debt-coverage ratio should correspond to the standard deviation of the income from the asset. This is beyond the scope of this book, but the main point of this is that the amount of debt should be capped so that the risk is manageable.

g. Make sure not to have too much debt against the asset. The remaining capital should be structured as equity financing. Refer to *The Wealthy Code* for more information.

This is your simplest framework for Equity Pairs. This pairing of the financing and the asset allows you to start automatically moving to the other side of the WealthQ.

Where's the capital structure "glue" in the above framework? It is in the details, the questions. For example, when we say "The debt must be long term and match with your holding period" and "The debt must have the lowest annual loan constant possible" etc. That's the glue. That's the capital structure. It's embedded in the details of the capital and the asset side.

Here's where it gets really interesting. When you combine the Wealth Pair framework and the Equity Pair framework above, you can have some fascinating things happening in your portfolio. You move to the "Receiving" side of the WealthQ and you generate passive income as well. Now you have the best of both worlds.

If you refer back to the WealthQ table, you will realize there is another built in secret in there. The interest row is for generating income (Wealth Pairs), the inflation row is for an increase in equity (Equity Pairs), the opportunity cost is for cash efficiency to do more of both income and net worth, and taxes is similar to opportunity cost!

FORCE	PAYING SIDE	RECEIVING SIDE
Inflation		*Net-worth*
Interest		*Income*
Taxes		*Capital efficiency*
Opportunity Cost		*Capital efficiency*

TABLE 15: WEALTHQ TABLE SHOWING INCOME & GROWTH

This puts you on the "Receiving" side of interest, inflation, opportunity cost and lowers your taxes.

This, my friend, is what everyone should do!

This is building portfolios that automatically work for you! There's working hard and there's working smart. This is working smart. Take the time to learn and understand the information this book contains then implement it, and start letting the system work FOR you!

Step 3: Pick the Right Vehicles That Meet Your Criteria

Once you build the frameworks, you essentially have a checklist. When you select the assets and the capital that fit your criteria you will have built a Wealth Pair to help you accomplish the result you selected in step 1. Step 3, picking the assets then becomes much simpler. There is no more guess work. The vehicle either meets your qualification for step 2 or it does not. No more random picking of vehicles.

Investing will become a lot more systemized and interesting.

* * *

The key was in building these frameworks (which you have in this book and my previous book The Wealthy Code). My mentor shared with me all his frameworks, and it just made my life so much simpler. Little did my mentor know the impact this would have on people around the country and the world! Many people have told me how much confidence this has given them to invest safer and smarter.

One of the biggest lessons I learned from all this was that the type of asset almost didn't matter, what matters are the characteristics of the asset; does it do what I want it to do to help me obtain the result I want? Many investors on the other hand "fall in love with the assets" (as my mentor would say), but my mentor would always joke that "owning assets is annoying, and those people that say they love them are lying, we just own them because they move us towards the lifestyle we want."

I recall walking into his office once and stating "I love real estate" as I grabbed a seat. I had just purchased my 4th property. Without a flinch, he responded "you love it because you don't own enough.

Wait until you own twenty properties" he chuckled. He went on to say *"These assets beat having a job, and they help move us toward a better lifestyle, but we do not love them. We love the results they bring, and that's why we buy them."*

I would later find out how true that was, but it is all part of the game. The fun part I would find out later is what you do with the free time these assets buy you, and how SIGNIFICANCE would play a huge part of my life—just as my mentor and Emile had mentioned. In fact, the quote from Oprah would start coming to life for me; "The key to realizing a dream is to focus not on success but significance—and then even the small steps and little victories along your path will take on greater meaning."

* * *

Debt Millionaires Know the Secret is In the Capital Structure

Hopefully by now, it's becoming clear that what drives this method of investing is the Capital Structure. Debt Millionaires know that, and that's where they focus most of their time. Putting the right capital structures (called "Optimum Capital Structures") are core to The WealthQ Method. In fact, while most investors think they know "deal structuring", very few do. For example, many real estate investors will tell you to put on as much debt as possible when buying a property for long term rental. "If I can obtain a 90% LTV mortgage, I'll take it all" is a very familiar belief. That's really the first sign of trouble. Debt Millionaires know better. The frameworks they build will dictate how much debt versus equity to take. These frameworks will allow the investment to move them to the "Receiving" side of the WealthQ.

This brings us to an important and powerful lesson.

When looking at any investment and putting the capital structure together, there are 3 layers of things to consider.

1. ASSET LEVEL: How does the capital structure affect the risk and return from the asset? This is the topic of my previous book *The Wealthy Code*.
2. PORTFOLIO LEVEL: How does the capital structure affect my whole portfolio? For example, do I have too much debt (debt-to-asset ratio, debt to income ratio, etc.)?
3. ECONOMY LEVEL: How does the capital structure on this one investment move me to the "Receiving" side of the "Financial System" and how will it be affected by what's going on in the economy?

As you can see, every investment plays an important role in all 3 layers. The capital structure has to take all 3 layers into consideration. The beauty of this is that once the framework is built, all of these are built into it automatically.

One of the principles of The WealthQ Method is that for every investment (and its structure) you consider, you should also consider how it affects the 3 layers:

(1) Asset Level
(2) Portfolio Level
(3) Economy Level

Hopefully you now see why the wealthy on the right side of the WealthQ think and do things very differently, and why they seem to build wealth easier and more automatically than the rest of the population.

Many investors might purchase one asset and the capital structure for that one asset is fine, but it skews the whole portfolio towards having more debt. That one transaction might be the downfall of that portfolio. It's critical to know how to look at each transaction in relation to these three layers.

Here's what the Debt Millionaires end up with:

RESULT (step 1)	CASH FLOW ("Income")	CAPITAL GAINS ("Growth")
FRAMEWORK (step 2)	Checklist of things to look out for and structure.	Checklist of things to look out for and structure.
VEHICLES (step 3)	Assets that meet above checklist and structured correctly.	Assets that meet above checklist and structured correctly.

TABLE 16: PORTFOLIO BUILDING SYSTEM

* * *

This information was overwhelming the first time I heard it. I recall taking all these notes scribbled on loose paper and reviewing them at home, and having long conversations with my mentor about them.

What eventually dawned on me was the realization my mentor had shared with me the most important leverage anyone can have — and the one you cannot do without…

And with it, you can build all the wealth you want…

Chapter Summary

- Most people approach investing by picking some investing vehicle first. That's the wrong approach. There's a more systematic way to approach investing.

- Every portfolio must have "income" and "growth" ("cash flow" and "capital gains"). That is the result you are attaining and considered step 1. In step 2, build a framework of characteristics you need to accomplish these goals in step 1. The framework to accomplish "Cash Flow" is called a "Wealth Pair", and the framework to accomplish "Capital Gains" is called an "Equity Pair". These frameworks must also move you to the "Receiving" side of the WealthQ. Once you have these frameworks, you can filter which assets (step 3) will help you accomplish the goals. Notice that we worked backwards into the assets (or vehicles) to help us accomplish your financial goals as opposed to how most people pick assets, randomly.

- When you combine the information you are learning in this book about the WealthQ table and the idea of moving to the "Receiving" side, and in combination with this 3-step approach to building your portfolio, you will start to realize how powerful this can be. The Capital Structure is where the secret sauce lies and where the "Debt Millionaires" focus on and excel.

Chapter Eleven

The Last & Most Important Leverage

"This is just amazing!" I smiled.

"George, what do you think the greatest asset is?" my mentor asked me as I pondered all the information I had just learned.

"Not sure. Real estate, stocks, businesses..." I guessed.

"YOU!" he said. "You are the greatest asset. Everyone looks at external things seeking the greatest asset to invest in, but it is right in front of you every morning as you stare in the mirror. You are the greatest asset! Invest in you because the wealth you are seeking will be generated from you" he said as he pointed to my brain and my heart.

"You are the greatest asset. Everyone is their greatest asset, but they never seem to understand that. If they truly understood this, they would invest in that asset more than any other asset" he said.

"Wow!" I exclaimed. "Another powerful point to ponder."

I then leaned back in my chair, looked around and noticed all the people around us in the restaurant.

The waiter wearing white attire is running around from table to table...

The young couple sitting two tables from us…

The older gentleman that just walked through the door looking for someone…

All these people I thought had no idea what just happened in this restaurant. All of them have no idea that they are their greatest asset. All this knowledge I was gaining would have changed the trajectory of their lives.

"What are you thinking about George?" my mentor interrupted.

I shared with him my thoughts on how this information could help a lot of people.

"Not exactly" my mentor said. "Most of those people believe they already know all the information that they need to know. It's called the 'I know' disease. Others that hear this information never implement it. They allow fear to hold them back. Yet others don't want to learn to think, they just want to be told what to do and follow like robots. They will never make it."

"In fact the most important leverage of all is the…"

* * *

So far, we discussed the four "forces" we want to work for us and not against us. There are other "forces" as well which we will not discuss in this book, but there is one that is the most important of all… knowledge.

Knowledge is the most important aspect of the Wealth Equation. No matter how much you implement the information in this book, without understanding how to THINK about your finances, you will likely end up no better and perhaps even worse off than where you are today.

The most important leverage of them all is KNOWLEDGE.

THE LAST & MOST IMPORTANT LEVERAGE

Your "thinking capability" is the most important leverage you can have. The key is knowing who you are learning from. Many people learn from others who think like the middle class or the poor. They learn about being debt-free and the likes. There is nothing wrong with that, but you need to know that it leads you to different financial results than what you might be expecting.

It has been proven mathematically that you cannot become wealthy without understanding and using debt correctly.

Furthermore, besides knowledge, what's even more important than the knowledge itself? The passing of that knowledge on to your loved ones. Many people build their "empires" just to find their loved ones or the 2nd generation spends most or all their fortune.

The most effective way to transfer your acquired financial knowledge is through the family bank concept. The family bank concept is a lot more than just money. It's an effective way to pass knowledge from one generation to another.

In the beginning of the book, I started with a phrase about being hackers of the game of finance in order to improve your lifestyle. As I mentioned, this has nothing to do with illegal activities, it is simply trying to understand the financial system well enough to find shortcuts to make it work for you. You can spend a year or two to find a "hack" and it would be worth it, because it would help you and your loved ones move ahead. But more importantly, imagine if you were part of a community that works together and helps each other move ahead, and they all share their learnings together. That's a community that exists today for the goal of living a more fulfilling life by leveraging these financial hacks.

There have been so many hacks learned over the years and this book is simply the "big picture", the WealthQ and moving to the "Receiving" side of the WealthQ. There are other "forces" that slow us down such as fees, unexpected deaths, lawsuits, serious illnesses, etc. Again, as you develop your skills in this game of finance, you will start loving this field, for this game is real and the results are real money that goes into your pocket.

You are the GREATEST Asset.
Invest in yourself.
Invest in gaining the knowledge that will help you, your greatest asset, generate the wealth YOU need.

One of my favorite things to do is gather in small mastermind groups with other like-minded people and discuss these things, discover new things, and help each other elevate our game. It makes for a more rewarding experience when we know that the main objective of doing this is lifestyle, not greed. It is enjoying nature and what the world has to offer, not buying more "stuff." It is enjoying other people's company, not competing with them. In a nutshell, it's about enjoying the journey of life.

Taking the time to learn, gain knowledge, understand and build your thinking capabilities, and then in turn passing your knowledge and experience on to your loved ones is one of the best things you can do. Unfortunately we live in a society where we initially trained to do tasks repeatedly to accomplish objectives for others.

The waiter is trained to serve customers, keep tables cleared, keeping drinks filled, looking at the tables they're serving regularly to see if customers are signaling them, among other things, all the while being friendly and smiling.

An accountant is trained to reconcile bank statements to the company's books, prepare tax returns, issue financial statements of how the company is doing to management, and prepare a lot of journal entries, among other things.

Most jobs are just like that. You have specific tasks to do and to complete as your part of a bigger system to benefit someone else.

But taking the time to gain financial literacy for your benefit and the benefit of your loved ones has exponential benefits. I have found that as you gain more experience and knowledge in the field of investments and personal finance, the rewards are truly magnified.

For example, when I first started learning about investing, little did I realize that I would learn about what not to do! Through experience, I was able to connect the dots looking backwards, as Steve Jobs famously said in his commencement speech at Stanford in 2005. His exact words ring so true *"you can't connect the dots looking forward; you can only connect them looking backwards. So you have to trust that the dots will somehow connect in your future. You have to trust in something—your gut, destiny, life, karma, whatever. This approach has never let me down, and it has made all the difference in my life."*

I have found that every piece of knowledge or experience I gain builds on my previous knowledge and experience, and each has a compounding effect for me. I could have never imagined being where I am today without the thirst to learn.

The challenge with a job and working for others is that the increase in pay is not commensurate with the gain in experience and knowledge from the years of working in the same place, whereas the economic gain is indeed commensurate with the time invested and gained experience and knowledge in financial literacy.

One simple example is the "Opportunity Cost" section in this chapter. Most investors on the left side of the WealthQ are seeking higher returns. But it's clear that the benefits from using your money more efficiently by itself outweigh the returns that most people are seeking.

* * *

That meeting with Emile and his grandson Emile III changed the trajectory of my life. I really enjoyed their company. We laughed a lot. I could see why everyone loved the elder Emile's sense of humor, and I could tell that the younger Emile's sense of humor was just like his grandfather's.

Over the coming years after that meeting, I would visit the same restaurant and remember that meeting.

The time at that lunch meeting had passed so fast even though it was several hours. That's all it took for me to grow fond of these people. I would become closer with their family over time.

A few years later, Emile the grandfather would pass away sitting with his friends around a BBQ having fun. It was sudden and unexpected.

It was after his death that I would find out even more what a great man he was. During his life he donated a lot of money to charity, but not in the usual way. He would get to know people and then he helped them no matter who they were... and he would do it secretly asking that no one share what he had done for them.

He helped over a dozen families pay for their children's tuition with no strings attached, and none of these families knew where the money came from. Emile told the principal of a school that he would help families out financially but he did not want anyone knowing it was him. Only after his death did the school principal share this information.

There was always a different spirit about Emile. He knew how to enjoy life. He was a good person with a great heart. And he was so loved and admired by so many.

In fact, one of the moving moments for me personally was right after his death when his wife handed me a box and said "Emile wanted you to have this." I remember my heart racing. I was confused. As I opened the box slowly, Emile's golden Cartier pen appeared. It was the same pen he always used in the restaurant. The box also contained a hand-written note that read "It is with this pen that I signed contracts worth millions of dollars. It's my lucky pen. It's yours. You earned it. Now it's your turn. Make me proud."

It was a very emotional day.

Beyond that initial lunch meeting, his message to me was always about the importance of financial literacy, about the importance of developing your "Thinking Capabilities."

In fact, one of the last questions I was able to ask him was "why are you sharing this with me?" to which he replied "One of my favorite quotes was by Dalai Lama XIV; 'Share your knowledge. It is a way to achieve immortality'."

That was so perfect. He achieved immortality with the ones he shared this information with… And now this is being passed on to you.

And I was determined to do just that, and pay it forward, just like he did.

Chapter Summary

- The most important leverage of them all is KNOWLEDGE.
- Financial literacy is critical to your success
- Financial literacy allows you to be a better hacker of the game of finance in order to improve your lifestyle.
- We have built a community of people that have the same goal — better lifestyle and less greed. Collaboration versus competition. Enjoying life versus accumulation of money.
- Always be working on improving your thinking capabilities.

Chapter Twelve

The Family Bank

During the years I knew my mentor, he and a few of his very wealthy colleagues frequently mentioned two terms "family office" and "family bank" often. I never bothered to ask about them, but I recalled Emile also mentioned them a few times.

I remember hearing that upon his death, Emile's family received a significantly large sum of money into their family bank.

I felt it was time I asked my mentor what exactly these things were. I had made many assumptions, but I felt it was important I learn some more specifics.

This conversation I would have with my mentor would again open my eyes to something completely new that could benefit the whole world. It was becoming apparent to me that the rich have a perspective on life and a wealth of knowledge and both are completely different from the rest of the world.

The one thing that struck me immediately about this so called family bank was that the people on the "Receiving" end of the WealthQ all seemed to have one.

This conversation with my mentor started with me asking him a simple question "So what exactly is a family bank?"

"It is by far the most powerful and important financial strategy that can have a significant impact on most people's financial lives anywhere in the world, and in fact will make the world a better place" he said. *"Let me explain why…"*

* * *

Let's start with a very high level question—what is a family bank?

The "family bank" is an exciting concept for the accumulation of wealth for the benefit of a family through generations. It is referred to as a "bank" because it mimics the workings of a traditional bank but for the sole benefit of a family. The primary reason and purpose for its existence is the funding of various needs of the family now and also for future generations. The concept allows for the recapture of the interest that normally would be directed to third-party financial institutions, as well as the passing of intellectual assets and relationships to future generations. The potential compound growth of your assets (financial, intellectual and relationships) from this activity makes this a very compelling strategy for families to adopt. In fact, this strategy, as a whole, with all of its benefits is one of the most powerful and effective strategies for families today. Actually, it is THE most important and powerful strategy for families today!

So let's dig a little deeper to better understand what I just said above!

How do you pay for "stuff" you buy?

You pay for it with cash, a credit card, a loan, etc. These are financing methods. They are also known as financing systems.

The family bank is just another financing system. It's another option for financing a purchase, except that you "own" the credit card or the loan company. The family bank is your own personal lending company.

But that's just the start. It's a lot more than that.

Imagine a "bank" owned by you and your family to finance all your purchases. But this is not a brick and mortar bank, it's just a concept. Think of it as a separate financing business that does nothing more than finance your family's purchases.

Cash, credit cards, loans from banks or individuals are all financing systems. So is a Family Bank. It's just another option for financing purchases.

There have been many books written about the concept being a trust or about insurance products, but they are missing the big picture. It's a lot more than that. It's like someone telling you that a race car is the steering wheel, or the engine. But obviously, a race car is a lot more than that.

A whole book can be written on the incredible benefits of a family bank, and this topic is well beyond the scope of this book, but I will cover a few of the main things you need to know.

You can download a more advanced report on this topic. Refer to the Resources page.

How a family bank works at a basic level:

Imagine having a regular checking account in your local bank in which you deposited $5,000. The amount could be any amount.

Then you designate that account as a separate "entity" in your mind, as a "bank" that you can only <u>borrow</u> money from, not <u>take</u> money from. We are all used to "taking" money from a checking account and using it. This is different. You NEVER "take out" the money, you simply borrow it and pay it back over time. With this account, money never goes out without coming back and coming back with interest. Never!

You never TAKE money out of your family bank, you simply BORROW it and pay it back with interest.

To distinguish this checking account at your local bank from other accounts you might have, you call this account a "family bank vault." There are other types of "vaults" for family banks, but for now we will stick with the checking account.

Again, every time you borrow money from this vault, you have to pay it back with interest. Furthermore, every time there's a need to either borrow the money or lend it to a family member, instead of you being the only one making the decision on what to fund, the whole family, or a committee made up of family members makes that decision. After all, it is a family bank.

I'm simply trying to paint a very simplistic picture here to start. As you will see, it becomes a lot more interesting.

When you borrow money from your vault (checking account in this case) and pay it back with interest, your vault starts accumulating money. Now you have a little more money in your vault to re-lend out (money from the pay back of the loan and the interest earned from the loan).

That in a nutshell is a family bank.

As you build this bank's vault (again, checking account in this example), you start establishing some "family bank" rules for the family to follow.

The family should meet on a regular basis (monthly) to decide which loans to fund. Family members can submit "loan requests" and these are discussed at the monthly meetings. If there is a need for an emergency loan, a family meeting can be called for that emergency request, but otherwise it's discussed at the monthly meetings. For example; your son Bob submits a "loan request" wanting to purchase a laptop for $1,800. The family decides whether or not to fund the loan during the family meeting.

It is recommended that once a year the family have a "Family Retreat" that is paid for by the family bank. The annual Family Retreat is a great time to share goals, challenges, successes and lessons learned and also to plan for the next year. This retreat should be filled with fun activities for all the family members, which will build great family memories. The retreat should also include wealth building educational discussions for everyone.

Again, that in a nutshell is a family bank.

But as you will find after you start and begin to grow your family bank it can and does become a lot more interesting.

Benefits of a Family Bank:

There are many benefits to the family bank. Here are a few.

Part of the family bank is having these regular "family meetings" mentioned above. These are where the family meets to discuss loans to fund or not for family members. These meetings include everyone, but typically the younger family members (under age of 16) cannot vote. By having all the family members participate in these meetings the family bank and the financial knowledge acquired by the family is shared within the family and passed on from generation to generation.

The Rothschild's (Mayer Rothschild) started this concept in the late 1700s. This is how their wealth has been passed from generation to generation, not only their financial wealth, but also their intellectual wealth.

Through these meetings, the family members come together often (at least once a month), and the extended family at least once a year or more. This brings the family closer and builds a stronger family unit.

Another huge benefit of the family bank is access to and control of money. The ever growing amount of money in the family bank gives the family peace of mind knowing they have financial security in the event of an emergency. Beyond that as well, it gives the family access to money for major discounts and good deals, and access to such money quickly.

Additionally, by using specific vaults, some of the money can be used to grow in a tax-advantaged environment earning 4% to 8% which the family can borrow against while the money keeps growing. Talk about using money efficiently. The average American with a college degree makes $2.1 million over their career. Approximately 25% of that amount goes towards interest alone, not principal and interest but interest alone.

By having the family bank, that interest can be recaptured into the family bank and not paid to some third party financial institution. Every family member, including you, each child, each sibling, and your parents can have their interest over their lifetime recaptured into one place. The amount of interest that is being paid out to third party lenders that can be recaptured into the family bank is massive.

The family bank also has some pretty advanced features which make sure the amount of money in it keeps growing with every generation, beyond what we have discussed here. This is beyond the scope of this book.

Why does the family bank work so well?

Many people incorrectly think that with a family bank, money is essentially going from one pocket to another. That's what I thought when I first learned about it. That's not the case.

Let's divide the borrower/banker relationship into two sections. On one side, you have the borrower who borrows money from the bank and pays it back over time. On the other hand, you have the banker side that lends money and when they receive repayments, they relend the money back out.

BORROWER SIDE	BANKER SIDE
Borrows money	Relends the same money as it comes in
$500k over lifetime	Exponential Machine (model VOM)
Recapture	Exponential Growth
Interest Rate	Yield (or Return)

Consider the above table. Let's step into the borrower's shoes and see things from his perspective. The borrower thinks to himself "I will generate $2.1 million over my lifetime, and pay close to $500k over my lifetime in interest alone. A loan will cost me some specified interest rate. With a family bank, I'm able to recapture some of that $500k." But that's only true in his eyes. It gets better.

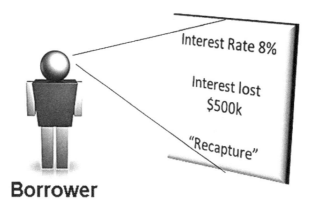

FIGURE 37: BORROWER'S PERSPECTIVE

So the borrower's potential "savings" with a family bank is as much as $500k if they captured 100% of their interest (difficult to do). But that's all the borrower "sees" — the amount of interest they can recapture. They are not used to seeing the banker's side.

Everyone that hears about the family bank can only see things from the borrower's perspective because they have no other perspective to relate to, and therefore they make decisions about the family bank without seeing things from the banker's perspective.

On the other side, the banker owns a money moving program like a "machine" called the VOM that takes payments from each borrower and makes them grow exponentially! This "machine" on the right side can make $1,000 grow exponentially to over $20k in 40 years at 8%. Imagine how large that $100k of the $500k a borrower now pays in interest could grow over a lifetime!

That "machine" is called the VOM, or "Velocity of Money" machine.

Applying the Velocity of Money process, you relend out the money, as soon as it is repaid, to other borrowers (or even same borrower) allowing that money to grow exponentially.

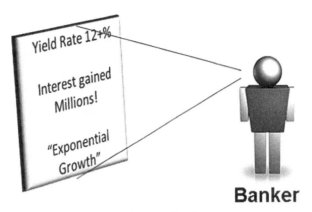

FIGURE 38: BANKER'S PERSPECTIVE

So if the bank made all that money from your $1,000, how much can they make in interest from your $500,000 over your lifetime? What about EACH of your kids $500,000 of interest over their lifetime? What about the $500,000 from each of your siblings, your in-laws, your extended family members, etc.? Even if the total of all those $500,000 interest payments was half saved and reinvested, that is still a significant amount!

Really, that's a LOT. LOT, LOT of money.

So borrowers "see" the interest they can save, but they never see how much the banker can make from that same amount of money because of the banker's VOM "machine."

But how does that relate to the family bank?

Well, when you see how much you can "recapture", it's quite a bit, but when you own the family bank, you OWN the "machine" that can grow money exponentially. Remember, you are not just recapturing some of the interest you are paying other bankers, you now own the machine, the "Velocity of Money" machine that can grow your money exponentially by lending it to you and the other family members.

So how does VOM grow your money exponentially?

First, let's describe what we mean by "velocity of money". Velocity of money plays a very important role inside your family bank. I like to think of velocity of money as the "turning of the same money". By "turning," I mean lending, investing, or reinvesting the family bank money as quickly as it is returned to or is available in your bank. When you lend money including the "new money" (interest) you earned on previous loans you are "turning" that money. In other words, that new money, as you "turn" it (you add velocity to it), you are using it to acquire more and more assets or profits.

This is discussed in more detail in my book *The Banker's Code*. Here is a section from that book.

So let's look at an example.

Assume two lenders, David and Steve lend out $60,000. Let's assume the loan terms are as follows: $5,600 per month for 12 months. Here is what their income stream schedules look like.

PAYMENT #	DAVID	STEVE (the smart one)
1	$5,600	$5,600
2	$5,600	$5,600
3	$5,600	$5,600
4	$5,600	$5,600
5	$5,600	$5,600
6	$5,600	$5,600
7	$5,600	$5,600
8	$5,600	$5,600
9	$5,600	$5,600
10	$5,600	$5,600
11	$5,600	$5,600
12	$5,600	$5,600
Total	$67,200	$67,200

TABLE 17: DAVID AND STEVE STREAMS OF INCOME FROM THEIR FAMILY BANK

They both started with $60,000 and ended up with $67,200 after 12 months. That's a 12% return.

David decides to leave his monthly payments in the bank until he receives all his payments. So by the end of the 12 months, he would have $67,200.

Steve, the smart lender, decides to 'turn his money' by lending it out as soon as it comes back. As soon as he receives the first payment of $5,600, he lends it out at 12% for 11 months, thus receiving $56 per month for 11 months (refer to the table below).

PAYMENT #	DAVID	STEVE (stream #1)	STEVE (stream #2)
1	$5,600	$5,600	
2	$5,600	$5,600	$56
3	$5,600	$5,600	$56
4	$5,600	$5,600	$56
5	$5,600	$5,600	$56
6	$5,600	$5,600	$56
7	$5,600	$5,600	$56
8	$5,600	$5,600	$56
9	$5,600	$5,600	$56
10	$5,600	$5,600	$56
11	$5,600	$5,600	$56
12	$5,600	$5,600	$56
Total	$67,200	$67,200	$616

TABLE 18: DAVID AND STEVE STREAMS OF INCOME IN THEIR FAMILY BANK

Steve ends up receiving $67,200 and the $616, resulting in a sum of $67,816. That's a return of 13.03% when David is getting 12%. But, Steve does not stop there. He does the same thing for the next $5,600 payment he receives as well, resulting in another stream of income of $56 per month. He then does a ten month loan with that money.

PAYMENT #	DAVID	STEVE (stream #1)	STEVE (stream #2)	STEVE (stream #3)
1	$5,600	$5,600		
2	$5,600	$5,600	$56	
3	$5,600	$5,600	$56	$56
4	$5,600	$5,600	$56	$56
5	$5,600	$5,600	$56	$56
6	$5,600	$5,600	$56	$56
7	$5,600	$5,600	$56	$56
8	$5,600	$5,600	$56	$56
9	$5,600	$5,600	$56	$56
10	$5,600	$5,600	$56	$56
11	$5,600	$5,600	$56	$56
12	$5,600	$5,600	$56	$56
Total	$67,200	$67,200	$616	$560

TABLE 19: DAVID AND STEVE STREAMS OF INCOME IN THEIR FAMILY BANK. STEVE IS USING VELOCITY OF MONEY TO MAKE MORE MONEY

Steve ends up receiving three streams of income: $67,200, $616 and the $560, resulting in a sum of $68,376. That's a return of 13.96% when David is getting 12%. However, Steve does not stop there. He does the same thing for every $5,600 payment he receives as well, which results in another stream of income for $56 per month for each one. He does that every single month, and in fact, his return percentage keeps going up as he continues to do so.

PAYMENT #	DAVID	STEVE (stream #1)	STEVE (stream #2)	STEVE (stream #3)	STEVE (stream #4)
1	$5,600	$5,600			
2	$5,600	$5,600	$56		
3	$5,600	$5,600	$56	$56	
4	$5,600	$5,600	$56	$56	$56
5	$5,600	$5,600	$56	$56	$56
6	$5,600	$5,600	$56	$56	$56
7	$5,600	$5,600	$56	$56	$56
8	$5,600	$5,600	$56	$56	$56
9	$5,600	$5,600	$56	$56	$56
10	$5,600	$5,600	$56	$56	$56
11	$5,600	$5,600	$56	$56	$56
12	$5,600	$5,600	$56	$56	$56
Total	$67,200	$67,200	$616	$560	$504

TABLE 20: DAVID AND STEVE STREAMS OF INCOME IN THEIR FAMILY BANK. STEVE IS USING VELOCITY OF MONEY TO MAKE MORE MONEY

David: $67,200 (12.00% return)

Steve: $67,200 + $616 + $560 + $504 = $68,880 (14.80% return)

The only difference between David, who is now getting 12%, and Steve, who is getting a much higher return, is that Steve is using the velocity of money. In fact, his strategy is simple. As soon as money is back in his bank account, he lends it right back out. Sometimes, it might sit idle for a few months, but he will lend it as soon as he has a chance.

In fact, if you think about the above statement carefully, you realize that Steve is even relending the $56 right back out as soon as he receives it, making money on *that* money as well!

Velocity of money increases your returns and allows your money to grow exponentially.

Now, the reality is that you might not be able to lend the money right back out immediately as stated earlier. It might sit idle for a few months.

So the VOM machine is used by the right side of the Wealth Equation, typically by banks etc. By shifting over and having a family bank, you now "own" this machine as well. But you will need to know how to run this VOM machine.

So to wrap up this discussion, a family bank is not about moving money from one pocket to another. It's a lot more than that. In fact, it's about recapturing interest from family members in an exponential way.

What we covered so far with the family bank is only the tip of the iceberg, the very tip. This is such an exciting strategy and goes well beyond the scope of this book.

In fact, the "Family bank" is a whole new movement and I believe most families should have one. In fact, I personally believe in it so much that we created a company with the sole vision of reaching one million people by Dec 31, 2020, and have it take on a life of its own. We decided to do that by having families all over the world teach it to other families. This is done through a live and fun interactive game played in huge rooms with many players. This 2-day game is meant to bring families together with other families and have everyone learn together. My personal goal is that this is talked about in every neighborhood in the world. Even though it makes sense financially, the family bank is a LOT more than just money. It's about relationships and the passing of knowledge and experience to your loved ones.

Anyways, I digress.

Again, there's more advanced features that are not covered in this book. I just wanted to share with you some of the highlights of the family bank.

Perhaps I'll write a book on that someday.

So why does this move you to the right side?

The family bank in addition to the more advanced vaults allows you start moving to the right side of the Wealth Equation.

Family Bank allows you to move to the right side of the Wealth Equation

Remember the four forces? With a family bank you become the recipient of <u>interest</u>. You are recapturing your own interest, as well as your family members' interest. On <u>taxes</u>, there are some tax-advantages of certain advanced vaults. Furthermore, the money in the advanced vault allows you to use the money in two places at the same time (<u>opportunity cost</u>). Refer to *The Banker's Code* for more information. In terms of <u>inflation</u>, the advanced vaults allow you to use the same money in multiple places using the debt to beat the inflation rate.

FORCE	PAYING SIDE	RECEIVING SIDE
Inflation		Family Bank used right allows you to beat inflation
Interest		Family Bank allows you to recapture your and your family's interest
Taxes	Family Bank allows you to pay less in taxes	
Opportunity Cost		Family Bank allows you to use your capital in multiple places and gives you a new financing system to tap into

TABLE 21: THE FAMILY BANK USED RIGHT ALLOWS YOU TO MOVE TO THE RIGHT SIDE OF WEALTH EQUATION

However, the critical point here is that you start your family bank. The primary power and benefit of the family bank is not the knowing the above process but rather actually doing the process. I strongly recommend you start your family bank with just a checking account and focus on doing the process regularly. Please refer to the resources page for more information on family banks.

* * *

That was simply amazing what my mentor described.

So now what about the "family office?" I asked.

"The richest families in the world have so much money that it makes no sense to have financial institutions manage their money. Imagine a family with a billion dollars, or $500 million. They can afford to hire some of the smartest people on the planet to manage their wealth for them. That is a simple explanation of how a family office works. If a rich family has $250 million or less, a few families might share a family office. That's called a multi-family office. A single family with its own family office is called a single-family office" my mentor went on.

"The family office invests in various investments out there."

"However, all these family offices have a family bank at their core. And in fact, every family can benefit from their own family bank. You can be in debt, no debt, rich or poor, you can hugely benefit from the family bank" he said.

Chapter Thirteen

Putting it All Together

A few days later, I walked into my mentor's office.

He was just finishing up a meeting related to some sky-scraper he was building in downtown San Jose.

After some small talk, I asked him to help me put everything we covered during the lunch with Emile and his grandson together.

It was a lot to absorb.

* * *

Let's review where we started.

We started by recognizing that the current method of investing used by the majority of the population and investors doesn't work. The math shows that before taxes, inflation, and after fees, the returns needed just to break even are practically impossible to attain, and more importantly to maintain year after year in a compounding manner, and that is just to break even, not even build wealth! (Refer to chapter three).

We then learned that the ultra-wealthy use a completely different method of investing called "The WealthQ Method" which challenges everything we know about investing. It goes against everything we have been told about investing!

This new method is based on something called "The Wealth Equation" which identifies people as either being on the "Paying" side and the "Receiving" side. Most people are on the "Paying" side, and that simply means the financial system works AGAINST them, while the few on the right side, the "Receiving" side, understand how the system works, and have moved to the right side to make the system work for them automatically.

In fact, the result of this powerful and advanced WealthQ Method is that the people on the "Paying" side, unbeknownst to them, are transferring their wealth to the people on the "Receiving" side. This is not done with bad intentions by the investors on the "Receiving" side, it is simply due to the investors' lack of knowledge on the "Paying" side!

Lack of knowledge in this case is very expensive!

Inflation, Interest, Taxes and Opportunity Cost. These are four of the major forces (among others) that investors and the general population on the "Paying" side have to "combat", and in fact spend all their lives combating these forces. The ultra-wealthy move to the right side, the "Receiving" side of these forces to make these forces work for them and therefore become wealthier easier.

The investors on the "Paying" side focus on higher returns, low liquidity and riskier assets while investors on the "Receiving" side focus on more stable assets, higher liquidity but with well-structured debt and equity.

To switch to the right side of The Wealth Equation, we recognize we need to use debt correctly. Debt used incorrectly can backfire and hurt us. Too much debt can really hurt us. Too little debt will only help you take a small incremental step towards the right side. One has to know and use debt effectively to switch to the right side.

By using debt strategically and correctly, we also shift the work to someone on the left side. The people on the "Paying" side have to work harder and longer due to the system working against them.

Again, lack of knowledge is very expensive!

We also learned that it's the debt that actually increases your purchasing power and not the asset. The rich focus on the strategic use of properly structured debt, while the average person on the

PUTTING IT ALL TOGETHER

left side of the WealthQ focuses on the asset. Those on the left keep looking for various assets trying to find the "right" asset that can generate higher returns, which in turn increases their risk.

We then wrapped well-structured debt into a bigger "container" called "Capital Structure." Capital Structure is simply how an asset is financed. In simple terms, this includes how much of the capital structure is debt and how much is equity. It is the use of the correct capital structure, called the "Optimum Capital Structure," that allows us to use the proper amount (mix) of debt and equity in conjunction with the related asset. This in turn moves us to the right side of WealthQ, lowers our risk, gives us the best return for the risk we selected, and moves us towards the result we are seeking in the most efficient manner possible.

I also introduced a term "Debt Millionaire" as someone who understands the lessons in this book; "The WealthQ Method," and how to use debt strategically to move them to the "Receiving" side of the WealthQ effectively.

The challenge with all this is DEBT itself. We have been conditioned that it's bad, it's dangerous, and it's fire!

Unfortunately, we live in a world that is very different than the 1920's. Money is printed in boatloads, with nothing to back it up except the trust of the people in the government. No gold. So many things are happening around us, and not dealing with this reality will hurt us. We are going to lose by ignoring reality, or even by "playing" with improperly structured debt and burning ourselves. Thankfully, there is one more option. We can educate ourselves. Don't just rush out and start accumulating debt as that would surely hurt us more than we realize. We should take our time and educate ourselves.

You can fear debt or you can choose to master it. You can keep working hard against the system or do something about it. Move to the right side. Your decision.

The WealthQ Method was built from the ground up with the existing monetary system in mind to work for us instead of against us, and it is through education that we can play to effectively play this game of finance.

Let's compare people on both sides of the Wealth Equation. This is really comparing the traditional method of investing with the method mentioned in this book, The WealthQ Method:

LEFT SIDE OF WEALTHQ	RIGHT SIDE OF WEALTHQ
Focus on asset	Focus on financing
Take higher risks hoping for better returns	Focus on better financing with lower risk and more stable assets for better returns
Pay higher taxes due to focus on nominal dollars	Pay lower taxes due to focus on real dollars
Pressure to buy assets with higher volatility due to pressure to achieve higher returns	Focus on stable assets with little volatility and higher liquidity with well-structured debt to achieve higher and more predictable net worth.
Whole system works against them	Whole system works for them
Thinks in nominal dollars	Thinks in real dollars first, and nominal dollars second
Little to no liquidity due to wanting "every penny to make money"	Higher liquidity due to the use of manageable leverage to build wealth
Looks at returns exclusively	Looks at efficient use of money, tax environment, financing, risk and spreads before looking at returns
Approach to increasing net worth is "buy and pray"	Approach to increasing net worth is using inflation, interest, opportunity cost and tax advantages to create an environment where there is some certainty in the increase of net worth
Less sophisticated investor	More sophisticated investor

TABLE 22: COMPARING LEFT SIDE AND RIGHT SIDE OF WEALTHQ

Where to Start?

This book's objective was to introduce you to a new method of investing. It can be overwhelming since a lot of it goes completely against what we have been taught.

So the question is where to start?

The best first three things to do are the following:

1. Start and build your family bank. Keep it simple. Don't complicate it.
2. Practice by analyzing portfolios and identifying what can be done to move to the "Receiving" side of the WealthQ.
3. Read this book again.

Again, you can start with a relatively simple strategy such as "the family bank" that moves you towards being on the "Receiving" side. This book is obviously a lot more than just the family bank, but this is one of many possible first steps.

Let's look at some simple portfolios and see if you can identify if these people are on the left or right side of the WealthQ, and if appropriate what needs to be done to move to the right side. This will help you internalize the information.

Examples of Portfolios
Scenario 1:

Kyrbi has $20,000 in her savings. She purchased a rental property with fixed-interest rate, 80% debt, with the lowest loan constant. She made sure that her risk metrics were in the ranges she set for herself. She raised equity-financing from her friend John. John invested the 20% down payment, and they agreed they would split all profits 50/50. She kept her $20,000 in her savings for liquidity and emergency. Here is how that one transaction moved Kyrbi on the Wealth Equation:

Analysis:
- The well-structured debt moved her to the receiving side of inflation.
- The renter paying rent in that rental property moves her to the "passing it" side of interest.
- Not using her money and structuring the deal to be safer moves her to the receiving side of opportunity cost. Having reserves is one of the keys to The WealthQ Method.
- Keeping her $20,000 in her savings account will help cover any emergencies, but also kept her liquid, which would help in purchasing another rental property in the future.
- Running this by her tax attorney and accountant made sure she is aware of tax implications of this transaction.
- By using debt correctly, she is on the receiving end of inflation as well.

Scenario 2:

Tobe has great credit. She wants to maintain it. So she purchased a car for $30,000 with her savings. She then used her remaining $10,000 in her savings to buy her living room furniture. She is very proud. She doesn't like debt.

Analysis:

By Tobe spending her last $40,000 on a car and furniture, let's calculate her lost opportunity cost. Consider what would happen if she purchased her car and furniture with low-cost debt, kept

$10,000 in a liquid account to keep her ability to obtain more loans, and used her remaining $30,000 to invest in an asset that paid 12% for the next 20 years. (Perhaps private lending—refer to my previous book *The Banker's Code*). The "Future Value" of that $30,000 would be $289,388.79 not counting taxes. The car in 20 years would be worth $0!

The debt on the car and furniture would not move her to the "Receiving" side since the assets (car and furniture) are not the right assets. However, that debt allowed Tobe to free up her savings to invest into the right assets to move her to the "Receiving" side. Her liquid account will allow her to handle any emergencies in the loan payments and maintain her ability to obtain more debt for moving her to the right side of the WealthQ.

The ability to look at various portfolios and analyze what can be done to move to the other side is great practice. I recommend talking to people about their portfolios and without giving advice (you are not licensed to do so), but just for the fun and practice, review and discuss their portfolios. Have them read this book, and this will make it easier to discuss. I make sure I do that with my students. Lots of "a-ha" moments are gained from these discussions.

And finally, read this book again. If you need further help, make sure to contact us. Our contact information is in the back of this book.

*　*　*

I was staring at my mentor as he completed his review of everything we talked about over lunch.

"George, snap out of it! Hello, anyone there?" he chuckled.

"You know what" I said slowly, "It's amazing how hard people work out there. They CHOOSE to be poor. They CHOOSE to suffer in their jobs. They CHOOSE to let life pass them by. They CHOOSE the pain of life, sitting behind a desk in a cubicle and bouncing all through life."

"What I have learned from you and Emile can change many lives, but so many people are just not willing to learn it or even open to learning it" I uttered.

I am a skeptical person, but I am very open to listening to new concepts. I just have to be able to prove the information right (or wrong) to myself as the case may be. I believe skeptics make better investors if they use their skepticism as an advantage instead of a disadvantage.

I knew I was tired of working against the system. I knew I wanted more out of life. I knew I would have good days and bad days doing anything new, and in fact more bad days than new in the beginning, but at least I knew what was possible. I knew I was moving in the right direction. I knew what lifestyle I wanted. I knew that nothing would stop me from achieving my goals.

I knew that I needed to step into my fear, because on the other side of my fear was my greatness.

So I took the step...

Little did I know that it would change my life in more ways than I thought!

Chapter Summary

- Move to the right side of the Wealth Equation
- The four forces we discussed in the book are Inflation, Interest, Taxes and Opportunity Cost. Make them work for you.
- Become educated on how to use debt correctly. Become a "Debt Millionaire."

Epilogue

As I stood up to leave my mentor's office, he hesitantly said "George... ummm... don't forget what this is really all about."

He turned towards his computer monitor to start typing.

I waited for him to continue.

There was an uncomfortable silence.

"Enjoy life. Enjoy the people around you. Enjoy your vacations. You cannot take money with you when you die, enjoy life. You have just one life to live. Live it" he said as he focused on his monitor.

"What we discussed is a game, just a game. We help one another win the financial game, but it's a game. Living your life with passion and making a difference in other people's lives is what this is about."

"We love to hack the financial system to support or improve our lifestyle and just for the challenge of doing it. It's a game George. Hacking the financial system means understanding the system that was setup by the bankers of the world, finding shortcuts and using them. Make sure they are legal and ethical. That's the fun part of the game. But as I said, it's just a game."

"The wealthiest people still struggle with happiness. They still struggle with health. They still have challenges. You know how to enjoy life, don't change. You do not need money to start living life."

"In fact, George, here's a big secret that most rich people will never tell you. They admire the people that live life now and take care of themselves. That's worth all the money in the world to them."

As I listened to him, I noticed a sign next to the door that said "When writing the story of your life, don't let anyone else hold the pen."

"When writing the story of your life, don't let anyone else hold the pen."

He continued "When you release money from being the measure of your success, and start living life, that's the most admirable quality. People will be drawn to you. They won't know what it is about you that is so magnetic, but it's the fact that money doesn't drive you anymore."

Don't make money the measure of your success.

"Use your family bank for what it's meant to be, not for the money side. Now, go on get out of here and go have some fun" he said as he smiled.

He was still focused on his monitor.

"...and keep throwing popcorn at your loved one in the movie theater."

He must have seen me at the movies!

Appendix

A Few Debt Metrics

In this chapter, we will briefly discuss a few metrics related to debt. These metrics will allow you to start to learn how to measure debt. Before learning to control and make debt work for you, you need to understand and measure it.

Interest Rate

According to InvestorWords.com:

"A rate which is charged or paid for the use of money. An interest rate is often expressed as an annual percentage of the principal. It is calculated by dividing the amount of interest by the amount of principal."

When buying for appreciation, consider keeping the interest rate on the debt lower than the projected appreciation rate on the asset. This is not required, but it is recommended.

Cost of Debt

According to Investopedia.com:

"The typical metric to measure "cost of debt" is the interest on the debt. For example, a 5% interest loan means the cost of the debt is 5%. However, one should also consider any tax implications.

To obtain the after-tax rate, you simply multiply the before-tax rate by one minus the marginal tax rate (before-tax rate x (1-marginal tax))."

Loan Constant:

According to Investopedia.com:

"An interest factor used to calculate the debt service of a loan. The loan constant, when multiplied by the original loan principal, gives the dollar amount of the periodic payment."

The annual loan constant is used when using debt to buy income-producing assets. The income coming in from the asset (measured as the capitalization rate) is compared with the loan constant and the difference is what generates "passive income."

Also, the loan constant is a measure of risk. A lower loan constant represents a lower risk since it offers more flexibility. A higher loan constant is an indication of higher obligation for the investor, which results in a higher risk loan.

Loan Term:

This is the time period over which a loan agreement is in force. Before or at the end of the period the loan should either be repaid or renegotiated for another term.

You should match your loan terms to your exit strategy. For example, if you want to buy an asset, hold it for ten years and sell at the end, then your loan term should be ten years or longer.

Amortized Loan:

A loan with scheduled periodic payments that include both principal and interest. For amortized loans, in general, you want to have them amortized for as long as possible. A 30-year amortized loan is much better than a 15-year amortized loan in many ways.

Interest-Only Loan:

A type of loan in which the borrower is only required to pay off the interest that arises from the principal that is borrowed. Because only the interest is being paid off, the interest payments remain fairly constant throughout the term of the loan. However, interest-only loans do not last indefinitely, meaning that the borrower will have to pay off the principal of the loan eventually. Interest-only loans typically have the lowest loan constants.

Points:

Points mainly come in two varieties: origination points and discount points. In both cases, a point is equal to 1% of the total amount mortgaged. For example, on a $100,000 loan, one point is equal to $1,000. Origination points are used to compensate loan officers. Discount points are similar, but are there to compensate the lender as prepaid interest.

Fixed-Interest Rate:

An interest rate on a loan, that remains fixed either for the entire term of the loan or for part of this term. Fixed-interest rate are usually better than adjustable rates due to the uncertainty with adjustable rates. Furthermore, fixed-interest rates are a better hedge for inflation as mentioned in this book.

Adjustable Rate Mortgage (ARM):

A type of loan in which the interest rate paid on the outstanding balance varies according to a specific benchmark. The initial interest rate is normally fixed for a period of time after which it is reset periodically, often every month. The interest rate paid by the borrower will be based on a benchmark plus an additional spread, called an ARM margin. An adjustable rate mortgage is also known as a "variable-rate mortgage" or a "floating-rate mortgage".

The Wave Machine: Debt magnifies returns and risk

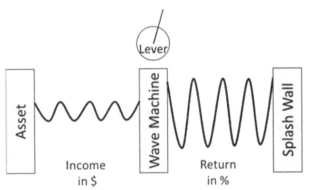

**FIGURE 39: THE WAVE MACHINE
(DEBT MAGNIFIES INCOME VOLATILITY AND RISK)**

The diagram above illustrates some important concepts mentioned in this book and my previous books. On the left side of the diagram, the asset generates an income (the squiggly line to the right of the asset). That squiggly line or wave shows fluctuating income being generated from the asset in dollars. Let's call that the "income wave."

The "income wave" then hits the "Wave Machine." You are the operator of that machine. As you turn the lever on top (the circle with a handle), the Wave Machine magnifies the wave on the other side. It the lever is turned to "off" (or zero), the wave doesn't change and keeps moving across the Wave Machine.

The Wave Machine is nothing more than the amount of debt. As debt is increased (lever is turned to the right towards maximum), the "machine" takes in fluctuation in the income wave and magnifies it further. This new wave that is generated to the right of the Wave Machine is your return (in percentage). As your return fluctuates more (known as volatility), that in turn increases your upside and your downside (risk) as is observed with the highly volatile wave.

So in essence, the income coming in from the asset, no matter how stable or volatile it is, is converted into "returns" and further magnified with debt. If the income is stable (as from an apartment building for example), you can afford to have more debt because although the additional debt will magnify the volatility (and therefore the risk) it will be magnifying the volatility of a stable income stream ("wave"). If you have a highly volatile income stream from the asset, then you cannot afford to have more debt because you are magnifying an already risky (highly volatile) income stream, which already carries increased risk.

This is important to understand how debt plays an important role here.

The "Splash Wall" on the right side represents the risk metrics you need to absorb the wave. So the higher the wave, the higher and thicker the wall needs to be to absorb that wave. That's why we have to consider the risk metrics whenever we adjust the debt amount. This is covered in *The Wealthy Code*.

Chapter Summary

- In this chapter, we introduced a few terms related to debt. It's important you understand these terms and how they work together.

Resources

The Debt Millionaire Basic Spreadsheet

You can download this complementary spreadsheet that contains various calculators discussed in this book at:
www.TheDebtMillionaireBook.com

Complimentary Special Report on Family Bank

You can download a special report on the Family Bank at:
www.TheDebtMillionaireBook.com

Upcoming Workshops

To receive up-to date information about upcoming workshops, please visit:
www.TheDebtMillionaireBook.com

"Family Bank Game" Events

To find out about upcoming "Family Bank Game" events happening around the country, visit:
www.TheFamilyBankGame.com

Interview: John C. Bogle

http://www.pbs.org/wgbh/pages/frontline/retirement/interviews/bogle.html

Contact Information

Company: FYNANC LLC
Contact: Support@Fynanc.com
Web: www.Fynanc.com